7137

ENGLISH MONUMENTAL SCULPTURE SINCE THE RENAISSANCE

MONUMENT OF RICHARD SHERBURNE, MITTON. BY WILLIAM
STANTON. (SEE P. 156.)

Frontispiece.

ENGLISH MONUMENTAL SCULPTURE SINCE THE RENAISSANCE

BY

KATHARINE A. ESDAILE

AUTHOR OF "ROUBILIAC'S WORK AT TRINITY COLLEGE, CAMBRIDGE"

"And monuments themselves memorials need."
CRABBE, *The Borough.*

LONDON
SOCIETY FOR PROMOTING
CHRISTIAN KNOWLEDGE
NEW YORK AND TORONTO: THE MACMILLAN CO.

First published 1927

Printed in Great Britain

TO

A. F. AND G. P. D.,

IN MEMORY OF MANY CHURCHES

VISITED TOGETHER

PREFACE

A MONUMENT is a memorial erected, privately or publicly, to commemorate the dead. It may take the form of a statue or a tomb, a mural tablet or an object of public utility such as a drinking-fountain, market-cross, or conduit head, but it is only in its restricted sense of sepulchral art that it concerns us here. The simple headstone, the stone coffin, the brass, are not within our scope; the chantry scarcely touches the period covered by this book; our business is with the altar-tomb, the elaborate monument, the mural tablet, with or without a portrait, the official statue or memorial, the historic episode, and what Horace Walpole calls the scenic monument, in which some dramatic moment of death or parting is seized upon by the sculptor.

For the earlier analogies of the sculptured altar-tomb, that most typical of mediæval forms, we need go no further than the terra-cotta sarcophagi in the British Museum; but the direct influence of such things is of later growth, and one remarkable difference appears at once. The Etruscan figure is alive, though its life is the life after death; the mediæval effigy is dead, and, in Ruskin's words, "laid dead in dignity"; it is centuries before it comes to life.

Such mediæval effigies are treated in one of two ways. Warriors in chain mail or plate armour, Crusaders all, in popular belief, lie with their legs crossed; the more normal type, whether alone or with a wife or wives, lie rigid in death, with hands placed together in the attitude of prayer. So exquisite are these recumbent statues, whether soldiers, ladies, kings or queens, priests or statesmen, that it comes as something

of a shock to learn that they are scarcely ever portraits.[1]
Types they are, but no more, and we must face the fact
and take them for what they are, great works of art,
often with colouring, complete or partial, to add to
their convincing quality.

The mural tablet is a curiously late development,
probably because, while knight or noble was commemorated by a noble monument, the modest brass
or headstone had long served those of a lower station.
Very few surviving examples are earlier than the second
half of the sixteenth century, but their abundance from
that time forward is evidence of the increasing wealth
of the country. The most interesting, as a rule, are
those with busts or kneeling figures, which, when they
belong to the English school of alabaster or sandstone
workers, are usually coloured to the life ; but tablets
which depend solely on their architectural quality are
very many, and often equally beautiful to the eye
which can appreciate proportion, lettering, and the
intelligent use of good material.

A chantry, in the words of the Oxford Dictionary,
was " a chapel, altar, or part of a church . . . endowed "
for daily Mass. It may or may not contain an effigy,
and where there is one, it is usually of great beauty
and in superb condition, even if the architectural setting
has been damaged. Chantries, in the nature of things,
are pre-Reformation or Marian, and they are almost
invariably admirable works of art.

Out of them, it would seem, arose the classicising
canopied tomb of the sixteenth and seventeenth centuries ; and so, ultimately, the species of classical
temple in which effigies from 1680 to 1770 are so often
enshrined. The official statue or memorial is usually
of later growth, but earlier instances, notably of famous
townsmen such as Hugh Ripley of Ripon or Richard
Watts of Rochester, exist to show the honour in which
they were held by their fellow-citizens. The scenic

[1] F. Crossley, *English Monuments before* 1500 ; *Enc. Brit.* (11th ed.),
ix, p. 10. The analogy of the Attic grave relief is singularly close.

or dramatic monument is naturally the rarest, and
indeed can hardly be touched on here. Its supreme
masters are John Bushnell in the seventeenth century
and Louis François Roubiliac in the eighteenth, and
with this we may leave the matter for the moment,
and turn to some general remarks upon the subject
of monumental sculpture and the species of problem
with which the inquirer may be faced.

. . . . . .

When we enter a church for other purposes than
prayer, we do so either to look at the architecture or
to examine some detail of its contents, brasses perhaps,
or screens, or monuments, in which we may be interested.
There may or may not be a local guide-book—and the
custom of placing admirable little books for sale at a
few pence is, happily, on the increase ; if there is, we
shall find brasses, screens, fonts, Gothic and Jacobean
monuments described with some enthusiasm, while
later works are usually ignored or dismissed as hideous,
pagan, or typical. That Plantagenet knight and lady,
stately and recumbent, that Elizabethan with his ruff
and robes, his wife beside him and their children kneeling round, are pleasant and easy to understand ; but
that man in a wig, leaning on his elbow in a long-skirted
coat or wearing the loose drapery which modern wit
terms a nightgown, that other man in Roman armour
for all he is a contemporary of Swift, what are we to make
of them ? Yet there was a time when such monuments were the supreme attraction to a visitor—
witness the Rev. Philip Parsons, whose survey of the
East Kent churches, in 1791, records his admiration of
works which the modern guide-book dismisses as
detestable. Is it not perhaps worth while to look more
closely, to learn how that reclining figure was evolved
from our Plantagenet knight, why that loose drapery
or grotesque armour seemed fitting in an age which,
like all ages, was after all expressing a genuine emotion
in dealing with the memory of the dead ?
Some knowledge of the history of sepulchral art in

England is necessary to appreciate them, and as that
interest was long confined to pre-Reformation sculpture, a general account of the subject with chapters
on the development of the later stages, and some explanation of their symbolism, may be found helpful.
For art is a whole, and to divide it arbitrarily and by
date into Good and Bad is as misleading as it is un-
historical. Even the epitaph shows us how long, in
the conservative world of sepulchral art, the old formula
may linger. Though Sir Thomas Gage was buried with
his wife at Firle in the last decade of Elizabeth's reign,
his tomb still bears the mediæval prayer, " quorum
animabus propicietur Deus " ; yet England had been
Protestant for over half a century. So too in art,
period glides into period with no sharp division, until
the age of formulas breaks the natural current of
development ; that development, those interruptions,
it is our business to consider.

We have already seen that, just as the Athenian
stelae bear as a rule not portraits but generalised figures
of the dead, so the mediæval effigy is with rare exceptions typical and not individual. When the portrait
proper came into general use in the sixteenth century
—and English mediæval portraits in our sense of the
word can be counted on the fingers—it advanced ever
more steadily towards realism. Where the earlier
" marbler " had turned out kings, knights, and priests,
the later sculptor made a careful study of all available
materials, often under the direction of survivors, and
sent his sketches to his patron for approval.[1] Death-
masks, portraits, and descriptions were used for the
making of many works,[2] and it is a remarkable fact
that, in the many surviving sale catalogues of eighteenth-
century sculptors, hardly a single monument is mentioned. Nothing, that is, except the tablet or

[1] I have seen such a sketch in a private collection, with the patron's
comments on the margin, *temp.* Queen Elizabeth.

[2] *E.g.* Newton's monument in Westminster Abbey, the statue of
Sir John Cass at the Sir John Cass Institute, the busts at Trinity College,
Cambridge, and the Swift at Trinity College, Dublin.

gravestone by the village mason [1] was obtainable ready-made ; nothing but the framework even of the common Elizabethan or Jacobean mural monument with kneeling effigies seems to have been prepared beforehand.[2]

The principle on which our fathers and grandfathers were brought up is, briefly stated, that Gothic monuments are good ; that Jacobean art—which elastic term often covers the whole reign of Elizabeth—is interesting ; that what follows is bad, though it is an odd fact that Flaxman, Nollekens, and Chantrey have always been treated with respect by the guide-books. The fact is, that there is good art and bad at every period ; and, moreover, the standard of bad art and good itself varies with every period. There is nothing more instructive than to compare the eighteenth-century guide-books to Westminster Abbey with those written by, and since, Dean Stanley. Even so late as 1816 Brayley, in his invaluable volumes, praises Roubiliac's Nightingale monument as one of the highest efforts of human genius ; Ruskin not fifty years later coins the word "Roubiliacism" to express all that was debased in art ; and the current guide-books treat the work as a mere piece of sensationalism. To Wesley again, as he records in his *Journal*, it was one of the only two Christian monuments in the Abbey, among "heaps of unmeaning stone and marble," the other, which shows General Hargrave rising from the tomb, being also by Roubiliac. Of the latter it is sufficient to say that it is thought unworthy even of a word in the current (and admirable) *Westminster Abbey Guide*.

What brought about a change so startling ? The answer may be briefly given : it is due first to Neo-

[1] Thus a detestable Sussex man spent a morning in 1727 cheapening his mother's tombstone. *Sussex Archæological Collections*, xxv, p. 193.

[2] The frequency of such motives as side panels carved with ribbons and strapwork, fruit and hour-glasses, suggests that these may have been stock pieces, to be fitted hereafter to appropriate figures. For the rest, compare the agreement of John Johnson with Paul d'Ewes (Chapter XII) for the careful directions given to a sculptor in the case of a work costing only £18 10s. in 1624.

Hellenism; secondly, to the Gothic Revival and its later ally the Oxford Movement; and to understand either we must first understand the history of the art against which they were a protest. But there is no text-book on the subject in existence, and these chapters can be only tentative. Of their inadequacy no one is more conscious than myself; and it is to be hoped that before long a scholar better qualified may undertake a history of the whole subject, and set forth once for all the history of English Monumental Sculpture. We need a Ruskin of our Renaissance.

KATHARINE A. ESDAILE.

WEST HOATHLY,
September 1927.

CONTENTS

CHAPTER IX

CHAPTER X

CHAPTER XI

CHAPTER XII

CHAPTER XIII

LIST OF ILLUSTRATIONS

ENGLISH MONUMENTAL SCULPTURE SINCE THE RENAISSANCE

CHAPTER I

THE SCULPTOR AND HIS MATERIALS

THE sculptor, from the nature of his art, is no solitary figure, but a master with a band of assistants varying in number with his success as an artist. The " ghost," it is true, the man who does the actual carving from his master's model, is a comparatively recent innovation, and the growing practice of employing him is spoken of with regret by J. T. Smith, whose father played the part, then a new one, in the studio of Wilton and Nollekens during the last forty years of the eighteenth century ; but from the first the less essential portions of a monument were entrusted to assistants, though assistants of a higher rank than the quarrymen who actually obtained the stone or marble. The state of the roads in mediæval England made it needful for the sculptor to live near the source of his material ; hence the development of local schools, of which more will be said hereafter.

The case of the metal worker was different, since a foundry could be set up anywhere. When William Torel, for instance, was engaged on the monument of Henry III, his foundry, by a perilous precedent, was actually placed in the churchyard of St. Margaret's, Westminster. Minor craftsmen, such as enamellers and gilders, were of course still more independent.

1

The materials most widely used, stone and marble, were both of native origin, and it was not till well on in the sixteenth century that the import of foreign marbles on a large scale increased the sculptor's choice. The use of Purbeck marble for tombs, effigies, or slabs supporting effigies of marble, stone, or metal is too familiar to need illustration. The knights of the Temple Church are probably the most famous examples of its use for full-length figures, but after mediæval days it was chiefly used for slabs, backgrounds, and the like, its dark background setting off an effigy carved in a lighter material.

The early sculptor, imager, or tomb-maker, to use the alternative titles familiar down to the sixteenth century, unlike the bands of carvers employed on architectural sculpture who went from place to place and made their workshop of the building on which they were employed, worked, as already said, near the source of his material. Thus, while the alabaster effigies of Sir John Harrington and his wife were executed at Chellaston about 1460, the stone canopy of the tomb was wrought at Bristol. The works of this Bristol school of carvers, which have been recently and exhaustively studied,[1] were all executed on the spot and exported to districts as remote as Cumberland, the East Riding, the borders of Wales, and even Ireland. One imager trained in Bristol settled in Shropshire and there worked for the first two decades of the fourteenth century,[2] and we may safely assume that every important mediæval quarry had its own group of imagers, and thus provided a constant supply of trained men, some of whom set up for themselves in suitable places elsewhere.

Alabaster, used for great monuments at least as early as 1337,[3] is a material far more important. It was, and

---

[1] A. C. Fryer, F.S.A., in *Archæologia*, 1925. This invaluable survey of the mediæval works naturally takes no count of the monuments of later Bristol sculptors such as Sidnell and Paty.   [2] *Ibid.*

[3] On John of Eltham's tomb in Westminster Abbey. Leland notes, obviously as a curiosity, a "tumbe *ex marmore calchedonica*" in St. Mary's, Leicester. *Itinerary*, ed. L. Toulmin Smith, i, p. 14.

is, found in abundance in Derbyshire, Nottinghamshire, Staffordshire, and elsewhere. Leland mentions
Axholme, where the layers were " of no great thiknes
and sold for a XII*d* the lode," Leicester, and the
" many marbelers working in alabaster " at Burton-
on-Trent, and a valuable list of fifteenth-century
names is given by the late Sir William Hope.[1] The
workers of Chellaston had a style of their own, and
other groups have been recognised by students, notably
that whose centre was York.[2] Nor is later evidence
lacking. Vertue, for instance, notes[3] that " at Fair-
born near Ladsham by Leeds are Several Quarries of
Alabaster—the finest is used for Images (to be cutt)
& Funeral monuments—for which are dug up pieces
of a Tun weight—sometimes two or three Tun Wt."
Small wonder that teams of oxen, sometimes twelve or
sixteen in number, were needed to draw the waggons
on which such works were carried, or that the axle
trees of the waggons gave way under the strain.[4] " The
best *Alabaster* in England," says Fuller,[5] " (I know
Reader, I have consulted with curious *Artists* in this
kind) is found about Castle-Hay in this county of
Staffordshire. It is but one degree beneath *White
Marble*, only more *soft and brittle*. However, if it be
dry fenced from weather, and may be let alone, long
the during thereof, Witness the late Statue of John of
Gaunt in Paul's [destroyed in the Fire] and many
Monuments made thereof in Westminster remaining
without break or blemish to this day. I confess Italy
affords finer *Alabaster* (Whereof those Imagilets wrought
at Leghorn are made)[6] which indeed *apes* Ivory in the

---

[1] The earliest essay on the subject is to be found in Edward Richard-
son's article in the *Archæological Journal* for 1853 ; other literature of
more recent date is indexed in the Art Library at the Victoria and Albert
Museum ; the passages here given in full have been collected by myself.
[2] *Archæol Journ.*, 1903, p. 239, and Dr. A. C. Fryer's papers in the recent
volumes of the Somerset Archæological Society's Collections.
[3] B.M. Add. MSS. 23073, 14*b*.　　　　[4] *Art Journal*, 1903, p. 290.
[5] *Worthies* (ed. 1811), ii, p. 301.
[6] Leghorn is still a principal centre for the trade : *Encycl. Brit.*, XI,
s.v. Alabaster.

whiteness and smoothness thereof. But such *Alabaster* is found in small *bunches* and little proportions : it riseth not (to use the language of Workmen) in great *Blocks*, as our English doth. What use there is of *Alabaster calcined* in Physick, belongs not to me to dispute." It is a startling commentary on the last part of this passage that the Somerset monument at Wimborne, of English alabaster, has wholly lost its surface owing to the practice of scraping the stone for medicinal purposes.[1]

Alabaster then was for centuries the typical native material for a monument. Barbour makes his Sir Archibald of " alabast both faire and fyne Ordane a towmbe full richly " [2] ; the appeal in *The Merchant of Venice*, " Why should a man whose blood is warm within Sit like his grandsire cut in alabaster," [3] was addressed to the groundlings as well as the quality ; and when the Duchess of Malfi speaks of " The figure cut in alabaster Kneels at my husband's tomb," the allusion would instantly be taken by the whole house. Howell in his *Tetraglotton* (1660) does not even trouble to define the word except in Italian, " Sorte di marmor fino " ; and literary allusions to its monumental use are past counting.

The Chellaston quarries were probably the most important in England. Fine blocks were sold by the ton as late as 1829 to workers of cheap ornaments,[4] the cheaper qualities fetching only five to ten shillings a ton and going to the Potteries. It was from the Nottinghamshire quarries of mediæval days that the school responsible for the familiar altar-pieces worked for export as well as for home use chiefly came. The quarries of Winking Hill, Ratcliff-upon-Soar, were also important,[5] and in Staffordshire alabaster and cannel coal were sometimes used in alternate squares to imitate

[1] This is the verger's story, and the state of the work fully bears it out.
[2] *N.E.D. s.v.* Alabaster.
[3] Folio, " alablaster," the form in common use in the sixteenth and seventeenth centuries.
[4] Glover, *History of Derby*, 1829.
[5] Thoroton's *Nottinghamshire*, i, p. 29.

black and white marble paving.[1] English alabaster was largely exported in the seventeenth century, but so completely had it gone out of use that in 1867 the anonymous and enlightened author of *Monumenta or Designs for Tombs, Wall Monuments, etc.* recommends a return to its use as an alternative to marble for recumbent effigies, and draws attention to the beauty of other native marbles, now, fortunately, more appreciated, though the stranglehold of the Carrara product is still a serious obstacle to monumental sculpture.

Some conception of the extent to which alabaster was used before imported marbles came into fashion may be gathered from an analysis of the principal tombs before the reign of George II in a single county, Essex, based on the invaluable *Ancient Sepulchral Monuments of Essex* by Mr. Frederic Chancellor,[2] with its 157 plates illustrating nearly 200 monuments. In a certain number of cases the material is unspecified, though the type almost invariably suggests alabaster[3]; in others more than one plate is devoted to the same work; and of the five brasses nearly all are attached to slabs of stone or Purbeck marble. Still, the results are astonishing enough. Seventy-four monuments are chiefly or entirely of alabaster; thirty-one of stone; twenty-four of marble, including several of touch[4] only; five of wood. Brasses apart, that is, alabaster monuments represent 74 tombs out of 134 of known material, or nearly 50 per cent. of the whole.

The more elaborate monuments were exceedingly costly. Vertue notes that the Earl of Sussex ordered one by will, payment being made by his executor Sir Christopher Wray to Richard Stephens, Mason—a fellow-worker of the Johnsons, to judge from the style and character of the noble effigies (p. 121)—in 1587 and

[1] *Magna Britannia*, vol. v (1730), p. 115.
[2] 1890 fol.
[3] There is therefore much truth in the recent jest in *Punch* (February 1, 1927) that the average village contains " a monument of the last squire but fifteen and his wives in alabaster." In some counties the proportion of brasses would of course be higher.   [4] P. 10.

1589. The tomb was to be " of white alabaster, touch
and other stones according to a plott [drawing] thereof " ; it cost £292 12s. 8d., and was " carryd from
London " to Boreham by road, " in all 12 cartloads." [1]
We may compare the cost of the Johnson monuments
at Bottesford. That of the first Earl of Rutland
(ob. 1525) cost in 1543-4, carriage and erection included,
£24 only, though it consisted of two recumbent figures
upon an altar-tomb and numerous weepers, the " rough
mason " digging stone for the vault only receiving
6d. a day and his labourer 4d.

Prices then rose rapidly. In 1591 " Garret Johnson,
Tolmemaker," received £200 for the " makinge of
towe tolmes [those of the third and fourth Earls] and
setting the same up at Bottesford " ; in 1611 Nicholas
Johnson indented to make a yet more elaborate tomb
for the fifth Earl for " one hundred and ffyftte poundes
of lawful English money " [2] ; and it appears from the
entries in the household accounts that these sums did not
include the " Inricheing," i.e. the painting and gilding
" with fyne riche golde," specified in the " Plott " or
working drawing.[3]   Such costly works frequently crippled
an estate for years ; it is probably not without significance that More's Utopians commemorated their dead
by a plain pillar. The sums later lavished upon the
tombs of Elizabeth and Mary, Queen of Scots, are still
unparalleled.

Alabaster plays a less conspicuous part in Stone's
abundant work, and after the Restoration becomes
rarer still, though for the settings of marble figures and
for mural monuments it was in common use for another
century. Possibly the purest sort had been exhausted
by the middle of the seventeenth century, and the fact
that the painting of monuments had gone out of fashion
would show up the defects of the inferior qualities.
Certainly it is hard to conceive a more unsatisfactory
effect than that of the alabaster, veined every seven

[1] B.M. Add. MSS. 23072, 7, 35a.
[2] Art Journal, 1903, p. 290.   [3] Plates V, VI.

MONUMENT OF THE FOURTH EARL OF RUTLAND, BOTTESFORD.
BY GARET OR GERARD JOHNSON OR JANSSEN. IMPORTANT AS
ESTABLISHING THE TYPE OF WORK ASSOCIATED WITH THE EARLIER
SOUTHWARK SCHOOL OF ALABASTER WORKERS.

PLATE I.

facing p. 6.

MONUMENT OF THE FIFTH EARL OF RUTLAND, BOTTESFORD.
BY NICHOLAS JOHNSON OR JANSSEN. THE RIBBON WORK PANELS,
COLLARED PILLARS, WINGED DEATH'S-HEAD AND CHERUB-HEAD
ON THE KEYSTONE OF THE ARCH ARE TYPICAL OF THIS MASTER'S
WORK.

PLATE II.

facing p. 7.

inches with bright red horizontal lines, which is used
by Cibber for his statue of Clement Spelman (p. 29),
and which forms a startling contrast to the beauty of
that used in such works as the great monuments of
Ralph Nevill, first Earl of Westmorland (*ob.* 1426), at
Staindrop, Durham, and the delicately lovely Bridget
Paston (*ob.* 1615) at Titteshall, Norfolk.

In the sixteenth century, and frequently in the
seventeenth, the quality of the alabaster was less important, owing to the prevailing use of colour. We have
only to read the Recognition Scene of *The Winter's
Tale* to see how familiar the process was to the audience :
Leontes must not kiss the " statue " of Hermione
because the paint is wet ; " Sepulchres," says Lyly in
his *Campaspe* (1584), have " fresh colours but rotten
bones " ; and those who applied these colours were,
to judge from Ben Jonson's words in *The Silent
Woman*, a powerful and independent body. " Gilders
will not work but inclosed "—hidden, that is, from the
public eye. " How long did the canvas hang afore
Aldgate ? Were the people suffered to see the
City's [figures of] Love and Charity while they
were rude stone, before they were painted and
burnished ? No."

The same author, however, shows that their work
was already beginning to be unfashionable, for in *The
Magnetic Lady* (1632) Rut, the City lover, cries, " I'd
have her statue cut now in white marble." His friend
replies, " And have it painted in most orient colours."
To which Rut rejoins, " That's right ! All City statues
must be painted, Or they be worth naught in their
subtle judgments."

Ben was a Court poet, and his testimony echoes
the words of Sir Henry Wotton eight years earlier :
" Colours have therein the greatest power ; whereupon
perchance did first grow with us the fashion of colouring
even regall statues, which I must take leave to call
an English barbarisme."

The City's taste for colour, however, remained until

the middle of the eighteenth century, though the writer
of Dodsley's *London and its Environs Described*, in
speaking of the Royal Exchange, thinks fit to register
his protest. " The statues in the several niches," he
says, " have been lately new painted and gilt in parts.
The painting is no doubt very necessary for their pre-
servation, but it were to be wished the gilding of them
had been omitted, as it must give foreigners of judgment (and such sometimes frequent this place) a contemptible opinion of our taste." Nor is the reason for
the City's preference far to seek. It is far easier for
the untrained eye to appreciate a cheerful scheme of red
doublet, white ruff, black cloak, and blue breeches, of
hair, eyes, and cheeks painted to the life, than to enjoy
a plain marble surface, and there can be no question
that the method was applied by the English alabaster
workers of the period with success. (Plate IIIa.) And
their appeal is still potent. It was an old country-
woman who in 1923 began a conversation by confiding
to the writer that she had come in from the country by
train for the first time, and then, gazing at a highly
coloured group of a sixteenth-century burgess and his
wife set in profile on the window-ledge of All Saints',
Worcester, murmured in an awestruck whisper : " Be
that Queen Victoria ? "

Something has been said already of the Bristol
carvers in stone, who, like others of their kind, developed into a school owing to the existence of the local
quarries.[1] Freestone and clunch, Caen, Ketton, Reigate, Portland stone, and in some districts the local
slate, were used in different parts of England, for modest
monuments universally till of late years, for more imposing ones at times. Taste, alas ! has changed for the
worse in this respect, and there are few things more
irritating to the critical eye than to see a churchyard
in Somerset or Gloucestershire with its grey headstones and altar-tombs intruded on by a glaring white

---

[1] Nicholas Stone's father was a quarryman at Exeter : *Walpole Soc.*,
1918, p. vii.

marble cross or angel, a harsh granite obelisk or curb. Remarkable examples of the use of stone for more imposing monuments are the Arundel monuments at Chichester and Arundel, those at Broadwater and Wiston, the Hazlewood monuments at Pershore, the Bosbury pair (p. 13), and the Berkeley tomb at Bruton, with its fantastic classic detail. The churches near Bath are full of tombs of local stone, the Carew monuments at Camerton in particular, though dating from 1640 and 1680, being almost archaic in design and detail, the later especially, when compared with the work of such contemporaries as Cibber, Gibbons, and Bushnell. Stone's occasional use of the material is rather surprising in a London sculptor of the period, but as a setting it was used well into the eighteenth century, and even in the 1740's a tablet here and there—those to the old gamekeeper Mossendew at Harefield, for instance, or to the Duke of Newcastle's gardener at East Hoathly—shows what could still be done in the humblest of materials where a patron's taste, trained on more elaborate works, had a voice in the matter.

The carvers in sandstone districts seem to have been particularly active between 1560 and 1640. The artistic value of their efforts varies enormously. Such a work as the bust of Dean Goodman at Ruthin is as crude as possible ; the monuments of Sir John Trevor Trevalyn at Gresford and of Bishop Bullingham at Worcester, with solid blocks of inscribed stone taking the place of the body, while bust and legs emerge from right and left, are almost comic; whereas the Hazlewood tombs at Pershore or the Bedford monument at Cranborne show in every detail the influence of the contemporary school of alabaster workers. Shakespeare's monument itself, the most famous sandstone work in the world, came from a London studio, so that the use of the material does not of necessity prove a local origin. Like the alabaster tombs, these works are generally painted, now in part only, now all over, as in the well-known Nash monument at St. Helen's,

Worcester, whose pink cheeks and aldermanic gown are startling in their vividness. But the sandstone school is rarely original save in its occasional eccentricities,[1] and we may pass on to other matters.

It is highly probable that the stately stone mantelpieces of the period came from the local tomb-makers (p. 18); and if the Berkeley monument already mentioned, with its charming or fantastic heads and its nymphs in shell recesses, is due to the fancy of a local craftsman, the neighbouring church of Wyke Champflower contains a stone pulpit which may well have come from the same source.

From the existing agreements of the Johnsons, Richard Stephens, Nicholas Stone, and others, we gather something of the use of foreign materials. Touch, or black marble, chiefly used for slabs, plinths, inscriptions, or decorative detail, was imported from Amsterdam; now and again an entire monument will be made from it, but it is as an adjunct that it is chiefly important. White or statuary marble, such as that used by Stone and by his assistant John Schoerman for his admirable effigy of the younger Sir Thomas Lucy (*ob.* 1640) at Charlcote, recumbent among his favourite books, Homer, Cato, Horace, Virgil, and Winter's *Ayres*, and for the interesting scenic panel behind, was imported from Italy. So early as the middle of the seventeenth century, when the taste for painted effigies was in the main a thing of the past, it had largely replaced alabaster for effigies, coats-of-arms on altartombs, and other important features. It is significant that in the agreement between Nicholas Stone and Lady Morison, dated March 3, 1628, it is laid down more than once that while the "statue or picture" of her late husband Sir Charles on his monument at Watford is "to consist of good and pure white marble, royally carved," "pure white alabaster" is to be used, as an economy clearly, for the figures of their sons and

---

[1] Such as the cradle above the head of one of the daughters in the larger Hazlewood tomb aforesaid.

daughters.[1] "Allyblaster," however, was specified for Grinling Gibbons's monument to Henry Newdigate at Ashstead in the agreement drawn up on July 22, 1693, except for the table, which was to be of white marble ; and as we have seen, it was also used by Cibber. Still, broadly speaking, the substance had gone out of fashion, and after 1700 the alabaster effigy almost ceases to exist. The desire to enhance the effect of the now popular white marble effigy by a setting of coloured marbles, black, red, grey, yellow, or green, led to their importation on a large scale ; and by 1785 Egypt itself was being drawn on for materials : the monument, at Stourton to Hester, the young wife of Sir Richard Colt Hoare, who survived her three and fifty years, for instance, bears a sarcophagus of Egyptian granite and an urn of porphyry.

This increasing use of foreign marbles, chiefly derived from Italy, Sicily, and North Africa, led to the virtual disappearance of native materials for important monuments. Where in the late sixteenth and seventeenth centuries alabaster was habitually used for settings even where the effigy was of imported marble, in the eighteenth such marbles were also used for the setting. Once the principle of the " pure white " effigy was established, with coloured marbles around, about, and underneath to set it off, the demand for foreign marbles was bound to increase. The trade grew to enormous proportions in the eighteenth century, as the sale catalogues of masters such as Rysbrack and Roubiliac and of the masons who imported the raw material bear witness ; and the time came when even in a stone country with a local school of its own sculptors like the Kings of Bath and Ricketts of Gloucester made use of imported marbles for their monuments. By the middle of that century, indeed, there was a certain reaction towards a fuller use of colour, as the later drawings of Rysbrack and those of J. F. Moore (best known by his Beckford monument in the Guildhall)

[1] *Walpole Soc.*, vii, p. 62.

show[1]; and Paty of Bristol in particular has a notable
fondness for a combination of white and yellow; but
on the whole the white figure with grey or black marble
setting remains the standard combination till the
death of Nollekens.

The use of metal for sepulchral effigies is very early
and testifies to the skill of the mediæval metal worker.
The primitive practice of covering a wooden core with
beaten plates of metal, in frequent use at Ur of the
Chaldees, survived to an astonishingly late period in
the effigy of William of Valence in the Abbey, the work
of a Limoges craftsman, though of the neighbouring
Henry V only the wooden core remains, the silver
plates having been long since stolen; but the triumphs
of the art of bronze casting are of a loftier order. The
Henry III and Queen Eleanor of William Torel, the
Edward III of John Orchard, the Queen Philippa of
Hawkin of Liège, the Black Prince at Canterbury, by
an artist yet unknown, the Richard II and his Queen
of Nicholas Broker and Godfrey Prest, the Henry VII and
Lady Margaret of Torrigiani, are only some of the many
masterpieces left us in this kind; and the Beauchamp
tomb at Warwick is proof that such glories did not
exclusively pertain to royal dignity. Bronze busts,
like busts in general, are a later development, but such
seventeenth-century examples as Fanelli's Sir Robert
Aiton and Le Sueur's Lady Cottington[2] in the Abbey, or
the Godolphin bust at Bruton, or Fanelli's Charles I on
the tomb of Sir Nicholas Crispe at Hammersmith, show
the dignity which such works may achieve.

The monumental use of terracotta may date from
Torrigiani, whose Dr. William Yonge, once in the
Chapel of the Rolls and now in the Museum of the
Record Office, remains a masterpiece. Very little
later is the superb architectural monument of Lord

---

[1] These drawings are at the Victoria and Albert Museum. A noteworthy example of their effect is the monument of Young of the *Night
Thoughts* at Welwyn, which may be safely attributed to Rysbrack.

[2] The figure of her husband was added by Fanelli.

Marney at Layer Marney; and the Bacon busts from Gorhambury,[1] like those at Lumley Castle, are a proof of the value attached to the material so late as the end of the sixteenth century. The rare seventeenth- and frequent eighteenth-century busts in that material were, so far as monuments are concerned, mere studies, and do not therefore need discussion here [2]; it is otherwise with two very remarkable Tudor monuments at Bosbury, which, though of red sandstone, are based on the characteristic technique of terracotta. The first, erected by Richard Harford to the memory of his father, John,[3] is signed in full upon the pillars, " John Guldo [or Guido] of Hereford made this Tombe with his own hande Ano. Dni. 1573," an inscription apparently without parallel at the period. The recumbent figure in cap and gown with hands together in prayer lies on a stately sarcophagus, curved and banded, resting upon the bodies of two facing lions à la Pisanello. Above is a coffered arch resting upon slender pseudo-classic columns, under which are carved three armorial shields; on panels below are pots of lilies and roses; to right and left slender panels of flowers and foliage flank the columns supporting the arch, and above the cornice are acanthus scrolls around a shield. (Plates V, VI.)

Opposite, on the north wall of the chancel, is the tomb of the younger Harford himself, recumbent, his wife at his side upon a higher level. His right hand is raised stiffly to his head; his wife holds an open prayer book. The sarcophagus on which they lie is of the same general type as before, but it rests upon tortoises with upraised heads, and in place of the supporting

[1] Exhibited at the Burlington Fine Arts Club, 1926.

[2] Portrait busts such as the Roubiliac Hogarth of the National Portrait Gallery belong to another category. As a rule, however, the later terracotta was a mere preliminary study for a work in a more permanent material.

[3] *Tumulus Joanis Harfordi Quem sibi Suus Filius erexit Richardus Anno Domini* 1573. Further details are given in another inscription: *Hic sepultus fuit Johannes Harford Hujus Parochiæ Armiger Avus Bridstokii Medicinæ Doctor. Obiit* 30 *die Augusti Anno Domini* 1559. *Aet. suæ* 55.

columns of the arch are two fantastic caryatids, male and female, each straining a piece of drapery across the breast—Adam and Eve repentant, one ventures to suggest with hesitation. Arch and pilasters are rich with vine sprays, and about the acanthus-framed armorial shields below the arch the artist's fancy has run riot in a mass of flowers, fruit, and foliage relieved by grotesque masks in the spandrels. The inscription is cut on the sarcophagus itself.[1]

Who this John Guldo was we do not know. That he was an artist trained in the Torrigiani traditions of terracotta is certain ; that he may have been a pupil, or the son of a pupil, of that sculptor who for some reason had settled in Hereford is highly probable. That he produced two of the most remarkable monuments in our annals, and did so in the material most nearly allied to terracotta, is self-evident. The struggle between the free imagination which finds scope in the settings and the obvious effort to produce rigid effigies of the traditional English school is not the least interesting feature of the work of this sculptor of foreign descent domiciled in a distant county and working to the order of an English patron. His is apparently the earliest use of the acanthus on an English monument, and details such as the egg-and-tongue and acanthus-leaf mouldings on the edges bear witness to a familiarity with classical models which can only have come from an Italian training.

London from the first held an important position as a centre of monumental sculpture. Nearly all the wooden effigies were made there,[2] works of the Westminster school being found as far afield as Cumberland, East Yorkshire, and the borders of Wales.[3] By the close of the sixteenth century the capital had become the home

[1] The inscription, not of special interest, will be found in the Rev. C. S. Bentley's *History and Description of the Parish of Bosbury* (1891, p. 66 and pl. xi), where the importance of the monuments is, however, quite unrealised.

[2] *Archæologia, loc. cit.*, p. 28.

[3] *Ibid.*, p. 23.

of English sculpture. Local schools indeed continued
to a much later date ; the Kings of Bath,[1] Paty of
Bristol, Ricketts of Gloucester, and James Fisher of
York are notable eighteenth-century provincials from
whose studios monuments were sent all over England
(p. 17) ; but more and more London itself tended to
become the centre of the trade. Its importance was
greatly enhanced under the settled rule of the Tudors,
when facilities for road and water carriage increased,
and the growth in the wealth of the country was followed
by the erection not of magnificent palaces only but of
halls and manor-houses, whose inhabitants required a
statelier type of monument than the modest slab of
the mediæval merchant or minor Crown official. Sir
Thomas Smith, for instance, the statesman and historian, not only built himself a fine house, Hill Hall,
Theydon Mount, but ordered his heirs to complete the
monument which he had also planned.[2] Sir Anthony
Browne, again, erected his own noble monument at
Battle, leaving blank spaces, still unfilled, for the date
of his own death ; and I have seen a photograph of
an unpublished drawing preserved among the archives
of a noble house with the patron's caustic comments
in the margin on the fact that the artist had made his
wives' petticoats short enough to show the ankle.

These patrons, the New Men of the Elizabethan age,
whose wealth was largely derived from the capital,
naturally turned to a London sculptor, whether they
required a tomb for themselves or a memorial of their
own beneficence in their unforgotten birthplace ; even
at a place so remote as Bruton the Saxey Hospital is
in the next century adorned with a bust of the founder
signed by William Stanton of Holborn.

Water carriage was in mediæval days the normal

[1] The last of the Kings, so the verger at Bath Abbey informed me in
1921, lived on into the present century ; but after 1800 the works of a
firm which had been founded by a sculptor of high powers became indis-
tinguishable from the ordinary products of a mason's yard.

[2] See his Will appended to the eleventh volume of his Works (Oxford,
1828).

mode of transport for a heavy monument ; the alternative was the ox-waggon,[1] and in either case the work was sent in charge of a member of the firm [2] or a trusted assistant,[3] often without the sculptor having seen the place assigned to it.   If this were so in the days of stage coaches—and J. T. Smith assures us that it was—it is *a priori* certain that earlier sculptors, receiving a commission from a distance, did not normally see the place where their work was to be erected.

But if the neighbourhood of a quarry, whether of stone or marble, explains the rise of provincial schools of sculpture, access to good roads or wharves was essential to the success of the London master.   The distribution of sculptors' yards is accordingly significant, and as little has been said upon the matter it is worth considering in some detail.   In the sixteenth century the Cures and Janssens or Johnsons, a large and prolific family of sculptors, settled in Southwark (see Chapter XI) ; in the seventeenth century Stone worked in Long Acre, Pierce in St. Martin's Lane, Gibbons in Covent Garden—all places then on or near the verge of the town—Cibber, whose private house was in Southampton Row, in St. James's.   In the eighteenth century Scheemaker and the Kidwells lived at Westminster, though the former later moved to Piccadilly ; James Fisher [4] and Thomas Green at Camberwell ; Nost and Cheere at Hyde Park Corner ; Rysbrack and the Bacons off Oxford Street ; the Carters, William Atkinson, and Richard Hayward in Piccadilly ; Roubiliac in St. Martin's Lane ; Nollekens just off Cavendish Square ; Spang in Little Stanhope Street, Mayfair ; the first of the Westmacotts, whose sale was held in 1783, in Mount Street ; the Stanton family, working

---

[1] *Archæologia, loc. cit.,* p. 31.

[2] *Art Journal,* 1903, p. 290.

[3] It was when Bushnell was in the country superintending the erection of one of his master's monuments that he found himself with money enough in his pocket to escape to the Continent.

[4] Author of a singular monument at Marholme to the Lord Fitzwilliam who died in 1718 ; possibly a relation of the later James Fisher of York.

MONUMENT TO JUDITH AND RICHARD COMBE,
BY THOMAS STANTON. STRATFORD-ON-AVON.
THE BETROTHED PAIR ARE HOLDING HANDS;
THE SKULL IS A SYMBOL OF HER EARLY DEATH.

PLATE IV.

facing p 16.

MONUMENT OF JOHN ROBERTS, TEWKES-
BURY. A TYPICAL COLOURED ALABASTER
BUST OF THE LATE SOUTHWARK SCHOOL.
(P. 8.)

PLATE III.

MONUMENT OF RICHARD HARFORD, BOSBURY.
UNSIGNED, BUT CLEARLY FROM THE SAME
HAND.

PLATE VI.

facing p. 17.

MONUMENT OF JOHN HARFORD, BOSBURY, BY JOHN
GUILDO OF HEREFORD. TERRA COTTA TECHNIQUE
EXPRESSED IN SANDSTONE. THE EARLIEST MONUMENT
IN ENGLAND SIGNED BY THE SCULPTOR.

PLATE V.

from 1640 to 1750 or thereabouts, all three generations of them, in Holborn. The masons, who imported the foreign marble then so much in use and distributed the English, lived in Newington Causeway, Tottenham Court Road, the New Road, Westminster, and Piccadilly; one named Dixon had a wharf at "Pedlar's Acre, at the Foot of Westminster Bridge," in 1775; others named Can and Bird had wharves at Millbank in 1768 and 1771. The masons' yards in Euston and Marylebone Roads—the New Road of our ancestors —are almost the last relics of what was once a great and flourishing London industry.[1] Conversely, when we find a work by King of Bath erected at Sompting, Sussex, in 1781, or works by Fisher of York as far afield as Lichfield and St. Magnus the Martyr, London Bridge, in the same decade it is clear that facilities of carriage from those centres were readily available, or patrons at a distance would hardly have given orders to a favourite sculptor.

If one commission were a notable success, others were apt to follow either from the family or from their neighbours, the monument acting as a sort of advertisement in days before art exhibitions had been thought of. Before the middle of the eighteenth century, indeed, journals both in London and the provinces had begun to be interested in contemporary works of art. Monuments or statues by men like Roubiliac and Rysbrack were discussed with enthusiasm in the *Connoisseur*, the *St. James's Chronicle*, and the *Public Advertiser*; the project of adorning the pediment of the Mansion House was discussed in the *Daily Post* in 1741; and the arrival of Roubiliac's bust of Sir

[1] Some of these sculptors will not be found in any book of reference, but I have cited no one to whom at least one important work cannot be attributed. From the habit of signing a monument with the sculptor's abode as well as his name, e.g. *Jacobus Fisher de Camberwell, William Stanton, Holborn*, much of the information here given is derived; some comes from sale catalogues; the rest from familiar sources. But on the subject in general there is almost no literary information available beyond a *locus classicus* on St. Martin's Lane in Smith's *Nollekens* and much as to the Hyde Park Lead Yards in Sir L. Weaver's *English Leadwork* (1909).

2

Robert Walpole at Houghton was matter for the *Norwich Gazette* three years before.

Some idea of the sculptor's position so early as 1637 may be gathered from the fact that a man like Stone could bargain with a noble patron to give him "bak agen if I should have occasion to use it" a figure from a countermanded monument.[1] The artistic tastes of Charles I reacted on the position of the artist, and to be not a collector merely but an active patron became the right and necessary thing for the great man before the Civil War. An interesting proof of this increasing taste for sculpture for house decoration is furnished by a passage in the Vertue MSS.[2] of a curiously modern sound: "Fannelli the Florentine sculptor who lived and dyd in England, made many Small stone models and cast them in brass, which he sold to persons that were Curious to sett them on Tables cupboards shelves by way of ornaments . . . this Fanelli had a particular genius for these works and was much esteemed in K. Charles I time and afterwards." The taste of the age, fostered by the King's example, could hardly be more vividly set forth. The immense chimney-pieces of 1560–1640 were another field in which the sculptor's talent was, as in the eighteenth century, freely employed. Tricks still betray the workshop of the Johnsons under Elizabeth and James as clearly as a mantelpiece may cry out "Adam" at a later date, and we have documentary evidence for Stone's "chemney peces" and the architectural carvings of the elder Christmas and of Colt.

Something may be gleaned of the social status of the sculptor in the seventeenth and eighteenth centuries. William Cure wrote himself Esquire (p. 123); Bushnell was disappointed when the courtiers of Charles II did not treat him with the respect he expected, and refused to work for any nobleman who had slighted him; Cibber, with the Earl of Manchester behind him, did not hesitate to put forward his own claim to execute the requisite statues for the Royal

---

[1] *Walpole Society,* vol. vii, p. 48.   [2] B.M. Add. MSS. 23072, f. 8*a.*

Exchange of 1667, and subsequently calmly wrote to Lord Rutland's secretary that he had promised his little son Colley " a holy day at Bevoir," where he was then at work ; and if Lord Burlington had got heartily tired of the airs of Signor Guelfi before he packed him off to his native Bologna soon after 1730, he had previously given him free quarters in Burlington House. Bird's death in 1731 called forth panegyrics in the Press on his " noble and lofty monuments " all over the kingdom ; we know from Vertue that Queen Caroline visited Rysbrack's studio in 1733 ; Vertue himself was for ever in and out of sculptors' studios ; and a writer in the revived *Spectator* of 1753, in urging his readers to visit Roubiliac's monument to the Duchess of Montagu (Plate XIV) before it is sent to Northamptonshire, proves that the lack of public art exhibitions was no barrier to a knowledge of some contemporary art.

A sculptor of this type dined with a noble patron as a matter of course ; Scheemaker, to Vertue's indignation, spoke his mind to " so great a nobleman " as Lord Oxford in 1738, and told the Corporation of London that he had " done enough to show his quality " when they suggested his making another model for the pediment of the Mansion House in 1741. Roubiliac, invited to dinner by a nobleman interested in his conversation at an accidental meeting, was greeted in the warmest terms when his identity was discovered ; and J. T. Smith notes that Nollekens's table manners were so atrocious that his patrons would not ask him to their table a second time. Scanty as the evidence is, there is little of the " poor, friendless foreigner " business, which Allan Cunningham suggests was universal, in the place held by such men in society. That they had a hard struggle in youth is most certainly true, but once famous, the sculptor was at least as well received, and far more widely patronised, than he is to-day.

The extent to which the earlier master-sculptor did his own work is well illustrated by the twelve years (1631–42) covered by Stone's Account Book. That master executed some five and forty monuments ; in eleven only is outside help specified ; and of these eleven, three *effigies* alone were entrusted to assistants. Nor is there any reason to think this unusual. The master executed the bulk of the work, usually leaving a large part of the mere decoration and such details as polishing and fixing to his subordinates. Where a son was available, he was usually among them : the elder Johnson had no fewer than four sculptor sons, and Stone two ; where no son was available, a former apprentice often carried on the business. Cases such as that of the Stantons, where the business passed from father to son for three generations, or the Westmacotts, or the Kings of Bath, the last of four generations of whom used to come to the Abbey to service in the first decade of the twentieth century, are many and interesting.[1]

How late the practice of the master himself carrying out the more important parts of the work with his own hand went on is illustrated by the story that Roubiliac, suddenly returning to his studio, was aghast to find a pupil finishing off a bust of his own in his absence. Fifty years later, Nollekens, when the modern practice of handing over the entire carving of the marble to an underling which he did much to foster was fully established, entrusted the entire execution of his statue of Pitt at Cambridge to a sweated assistant ; Wilton did not even translate his own drawings for the Somerset House sculptures into clay, or carve his own designs for his General Wolfe ; and their example has been widely followed. Partly the change was due to improvements in mechanical appliances, the pointing instrument especially. Bacon invented one ; Chantrey improved upon it ; and the result was to make easier the work of the " ghost " It was unusual for any work

[1] The William Byrd who signs the Fettiplace monuments (p. 133) may well have been the father of Francis, who appears at Oxford early in his career as Wren's assistant. Can the Edward Peirce or Pierce of Deptford who signs a number of monuments from 1760 to 1787 be a grandson of his namesake, Wren's assistant ? I have seen his work at East Grinstead, Dover, East Hoathly, and Frant.

later than 1800 to be more than touched on by its nominal sculptor. While Wilton and Nollekens could rely on the services of Adkins and Nathaniel Smith, trained as they had been upon Roubiliac's methods, things went pretty well ; but their later works show the progressive deterioration which might be expected from the inferior carvers they then employed, and from the increasing dependence on drill and polish for effect. The modelling grows steadily poorer ; we have only to compare Chantrey's first bust of Sir Walter Scott with the later replicas to see how great that difference was ; and Chantrey's work, though it is against all traditional canons of criticism to say so, is often inferior to that not of Roubiliac only but of Rysbrack or Scheemaker, whom Flaxman airily dismissed as " mere workmen." But Wilton, Nollekens, and Chantrey himself in his early sepulchral groups at Hafod and Ilam, carry on the traditions of the Renaissance : that style therefore can hardly be said to have expired before the reign of George IV.

Each sculptor had his own method of treating marble surfaces, his own receipt for polishing, and that polish was much more akin to the old Greek process of *circumlitio* than to the sugary surfaces of the modern monument of inferior Carrara as prepared to-day for the English market. When we consider this elaborate preparation of a surface already carved by the master himself and not by an underling, we may form some idea of the reasons underlying the superiority of pre-Regency sculpture, and incidentally of the artistic inferiority of works of later date.

One last question, that of training, may profitably close this chapter. There never was a period when foreign artists did not find work and patrons in England, but the practice of English-born artists going abroad to study seems to have begun in the seventeenth century. The younger Stone went to Rome, as Bushnell had done before him, only his was a tour, not a self-exile ; Bird, Scheemaker, and many more followed their example.

All were master-sculptors, and in their workshops the sculptors of the next generation were trained before they too, if they were lucky, went abroad.   As early as 1752 there was an academy for English artists in Rome ; and, once our Royal Academy was established, a Roman training was looked on as essential.   Bacon, who never left England, was a marked exception ; yet such was his fame that Houdon visited his studio as Canova later visited his son's.   Even such a purely secondary figure as Nathaniel Smith could give Banks letters of introduction in Rome, and it was Houdon's visit to Bacon which enabled him to pass off as his own the pointing instrument invented and given him by the Englishman.   Both in England and abroad there was an artistic *camaraderie* ; and—more important still— English sculpture had become a profession, not a craft, much earlier than is commonly supposed.

But if our sculptors visited Rome for training, the training they received before the days of Winckelmann was catholic indeed.   Cibber, Bird, and Scheemaker, who all finished their studies there, devoted impartial attention to the ancients and the baroque, as we know from the models which they copied and the casts which they possessed ;   therefore they borrowed from both. All worked in England ;   all rank as English artists ; and English traditions as well as Roman are therefore embodied in their monuments.

The excellence of English carving, moreover, was world-famous.   Banks might declare to Wilton that " the Italians beat us hollow " in the art, but it was English carvers, not Italian, whom Sidi Mahommed, Emperor of Morocco, asked for in a letter dated September 1766, in which he begs George III " to send us an engineer with ten workmen in marble, all clever in their profession " [1] ;   and over a century earlier English

---

[1] *Catalogue of the Record Office Museum* (10th ed., 1925), p. 30, no. 111. A work on the various marbles used, with over 100 coloured plates, was published at Amsterdam by J. C. Sepp in 1776, and may be seen both in Dutch and in the English translation at the Victoria and Albert Museum.

artists are traditionally said to have been employed on the Taj Mahal.   Such tributes are eloquent of the value attached to English work abroad, examples of which must have been familiar in the East in the neglected graveyards of Tangier, Aleppo, and Constantinople, wherever, indeed, the great trading companies of England had either depots or representatives.   India and the West Indies also are full of examples of the art of English sculptors, and a comprehensive list of Colonial monuments of the seventeenth, eighteenth, and early nineteenth centuries is among the many *desiderata* of the student of English sculpture.

CHAPTER II

THE SYMBOLISM OF OUR LATER MONUMENTS

MEDIÆVAL tombs, like mediæval buildings, are full of imagery. The attitude of the stiff recumbent figure symbolises the body laid out for burial; its very character, typical, not iconic, suggests the office or station of the dead. Patron saints, weepers, whether human or angelic, remind us of their lives and creeds ; and such subjects as the reception of the soul into Heaven or the angelic Weighing of the Soul give us a glimpse of the traditional symbolism of the after-life. There is history, too, of course, and always the most determined realism of costume ; and for accessories, the very tilting helmet at a knight's feet may suggest, by the Saracen which forms the crest, his service or his fathers' against the enemies of the Cross, as the lap-dog at a lady's feet or the hound at her lord's take us to their daily life. A chantry such as Prince Arthur's at Worcester may be an epitome of English thought, the very choice of patron saints about a tomb suggesting perils past or deeds achieved under high auspices. Every cathedral will illustrate this permeating symbolism, but that of our later monuments is in need of interpretation to-day, when Roubiliac's Eloquence bewailing the Duke of Argyll is merely perplexing to a generation which remembers him for Jeanie Deans's sake, but has forgotten that he was the Chrysostom of the Upper House. The mourning monks who cluster round William of Wykeham are concrete, comprehensible, a true expression of the age of Chaucer, who, dying four years before William of Wykeham, wrote of

> Curious portraytures
> And queynte maner of figures
> Of olde work ;

for the literary counterpart of Roubiliac's work we
must go to James Thomson, who equally expressed the
spirit of the age when he sang how

Her loved Campbell sad Suadela mourns.

The contrast—the vivid detail of the earlier poet, the
shadowy allegory of the later—is echoed by the contrast
in sepulchral art, save that <i>Suadela</i> (an <i>ad hoc</i> Latinism
for Peitho) is much more alive on the tomb than in the
poem.   This literary parallel—and we shall return to the
subject of such parallels elsewhere—may serve to show
how art and literature explain each other, and help us
to realise that to judge one age by the standards of
another is a proceeding neither helpful nor intelligent.

Religious imagery other than generalised figures of
saints and angels is rare in English monuments after
1530.   Christ Himself appears above Torrigiani's
effigy of Dr. Yonge from the Chapel of the Rolls, and
there is a remarkable group of West Sussex tombs of
the first half of the sixteenth century at Wiston, West
Wittering, West Hampnett, and Selsey, all commemorating men who died between 1523 and 1545, which is
worthy of special study.   The first is a canopied altar-
tomb with reliefs representing the Annunciation and
the Resurrection ;   the second, dealt with in detail
in the chapter on Costume, has kneeling figures right
and left of a representation of the Trinity ;   on the
third are recumbent figures with patron saints, St. George
and St. Agatha, behind.   Why these monuments should
have been considered Italian it is hard to see.   The
details are English Perpendicular, and if the Bernardi
family had not settled in Chichester about this time,
we should probably have heard nothing of Italian influence.   Their marked and linear style is as striking
as their religious character, and their dates show how
little effect the Reformation, officially complete in 1538,
produced in the remoter corners of England.[1]

---

[1] A fine monument at Broadwater, near Worthing, somewhat farther
east, covered up when still unfinished and recently revealed, shows us
a fine sixteenth-century Virgin and Child and attendant saints.

No type of mediæval monument is more illuminating than the familiar cadaver, or corpse in various stages of decay. This grim *memento mori* was a solemn warning to the living, and it is significant that it appears to be virtually confined to important ecclesiastics. When, as in the case of Archbishop Chichele at Canterbury, it is placed beneath the effigy of the dead man laid out for burial in all the pomp of ecclesiastical splendour, the moral is only the more pointedly enforced. But though the cadaver had fallen into disuse by the middle of the sixteenth century, death in its physical aspect was not lost sight of, as indeed it hardly could be when the penalty of Adam's transgression was at least as prominent in the teaching of the Reformers as in that of the Roman Church. The skeleton, the skull, or skull and crossbones, the charnel-house itself, all play their part on monuments, both civil and ecclesiastical, although they had ceased to be the central idea and were degraded to the condition of accessories. Under the altar-tomb of Sir John Posthumus Sydenham (*ob.* 1626) at Brimpton, Dorset, for instance, a mass of skulls and bones appears under the supporting arches ; and if Colt's great monument to the first Lord Salisbury at Hatfield (Plate VII) portrays the counsellor of Elizabeth in robes of state, a skeleton in the same posture on the marble slab below shows to what complexion we shall come at last. *Hamlet* has been annotated even to weariness ; yet only familiarity with Elizabethan and Jacobean monuments—perhaps the only evidence not drawn on by Shakespearean editors—will fully explain how natural was the scene with Yorick's skull. The skull may lie in the hand of a dead man or under his foot or pillow ; it may form part of the monument itself, either as an ornament on the cornice, sculptured in relief upon a panel, or held by an attendant cherub or other allegorical figure. Examples could be cited by the hundred, from the sixteenth century down to the great monuments by J. Rose at Reigate (1731) and by John Nost at Sher-

MONUMENT OF THE FIRST EARL OF SALISBURY, BISHOP'S HATFIELD, BY MAXIMILIAN COLT. A CARDINAL EXAMPLE OF THE TOMB WITH FIGURES OF THE VIRTUES. FORTITUDE AND TEMPERANCE, TRUTH AND JUSTICE, AS CONCEIVED IN SHAKESPEARE'S DAY.

PLATE VII.

facing p. 26.

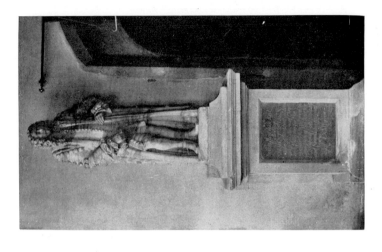

CLEMENT SPELMAN, NARBOROUGH. 'BY
C. G. CIBBER. AN EARLY EXAMPLE OF
THE STANDING FIGURE IN CONTEMPOR-
ARY DRESS.

PLATE IX.

facing p. 27.

MONUMENT OF VISCOUNT MORDAUNT, FULHAM.
BY JOHN BUSHNELL. A TYPICAL WORK
SHOWING THE BERNINESQUE TREATMENT OF
THE DRAPERIES AND ARRESTED MOVEMENT
CHARACTERISTIC OF THE SCULPTOR. (p. 13r.)

PLATE VIII.

borne (1716), or those other unsigned works, at Wanstead and at Mitton, the first of which, that of Sir Josiah Child, makes a finely decorative use of skull and crossbones on the panels, while the second shows the last of the Shirburnes, a child of many hopes, starting back from the sight of these emblems of his early fate.[1] On mural monuments they survive as late as 1785 ; on the village headstone for nearly a century longer.

The figure in its shroud, either at rest or in the act of rising at the summons of the Last Trump, was a modified and humaner form of the cadaver. The most famous example of the first is Nicholas Stone's effigy of Dr. Donne, the poet-Dean of St. Paul's, which escaped the Fire of London and remains the most impressive relic of the old cathedral ; a variant shows us a single figure or husband and wife side by side in a great vault with doors flung wide, a conception we may owe to the Marshall family (p. 136). Much commoner is the shrouded figure rising with uplifted hands, as at Old Chelsea Church, at Amersham, and in St. Giles's, Cripplegate, where Justice Shallow's daughter Constance Lucy thus answers the dread summons. Thomas Marsham (*ob.* 1638) again, at Stratton, Norfolk, starts from the sarcophagus on which he reclines above a grated charnel-house inscribed *Trophæa Mortis* ; and Egham contains a yet more original conception, of which more hereafter.[2] There, in the incongruous surroundings of a church of the Greek Revival as understood by Thomas Hope of Deepdene, stands, dirty and neglected, above the backstairs leading to the galleries, the amazing monument of Sir John Denham, father of the poet. The dead man, from whom the grave-clothes fall, is starting into a sitting posture, his left hand upraised to greet the summons. Below him

[1] For the attribution of these works to John Nost I am responsible ; it is based on the stylistic details of the signed monument at Sherborne and that of the Duke and Duchess of Queensberry at Durisdeer, the receipts for which are in existence.

[2] For the photograph here reproduced (Plate XXVII) I am indebted to Mr. Frederick Turner.

a frieze of skeletons and corpses, among them one yet wholly human head, start up side by side, with a strange intensity of joy.[1] Sometimes this intensity may be expressed on a very small scale, as on the monument of Henry D'Arcy at Hengrave, Suffolk, where below a superb kneeling figure of the dead man a skeleton, a tiny pendant finial, rises with hands outstretched, the shroud falling back from the finger-tips to reveal and frame the whole minute and delicate anatomy. Even so late as 1679 the shrouded figure of Sir Ralph Bovey at Longstowe, near Cambridge, rises to seize an anchor let down from above.

One strange and belated survival of the skeleton may be noticed before we pass to the subject of the cherub. This is at Quainton, Bucks, where on the sides of an altar-tomb surmounted by recumbent effigies of the Winwoods in the full Court costume of William III are incised two skeletons in the same posture. Imagery natural in the age of the *Anatomy of Melancholy* strikes us as incongruous in that of Congreve ; Addison's meditations among the tombs at Westminster did not include the charnel-house, though it appears in full force a generation earlier on the base of the fire-scorched altar-tomb of Archbishop Sheldon by Bonne and Latham at Croydon, under a mitred figure striking in its realism.

Why such conceptions suited the age of Donne and Burton, whether the long-previous period of settled peace had freed men's mind to dwell on metaphysical speculations which can hardly coexist with the practical risks of an unsettled country, is a subject which might well engage the attention of the historian. The fact is certain, as certain as that, after the Reformation, the skeleton was degraded to the position of a mere accessory, till the Nightingale monument showed him

[1] This vision of the glorified body is most fully worked out by Roubiliac a century later, in the monuments of Mary Myddelton and General Hargrave. But the *macabre* is altogether lacking in these great conceptions, whose keynote is the joy of the Resurrection.

as the dread Conqueror of Life, even in the works of that master of the *macabre*, the elder Cibber, as we see in the book of drawings which reveals him as the author of some of the finest monuments of the age.[1] Cibber had a love of the morbid amounting almost to a mania, which his patrons evidently did not share. His Clement Spelman of Narborough (Plate IX), a plain statue on a plain pedestal as we see it, is in the original drawing set in an elaborately draped niche, with angels holding a laurel crown above his head. On his right a figure of Time gazes regretfully at an hour-glass ; on his left a skeleton Death, dart in hand, weeps over his sad duty and wipes his eyes with his share of the drapery. To compare the actual statue, which corresponds almost line for line with the drawing, with the monumental setting devised for it is to see to what depths of absurdity the passion for gloomy allegory could descend ; but though the incredible conception of a skeleton wiping the tears from its eyes is several times repeated in the volume, I have yet to come across an instance carried out in stone or marble. The taste of Cibber's patrons was better than his own.

Not unnaturally, Cibber appreciated the minor accessories of skulls, crossbones, and death's-head cherubs, if we may so christen the winged skull so often combined with the normal cherub on a single monument as an appropriate complement and contrast. Its wings are bat-like, not feathered, and whether folded or extended, whether wrought in one piece like a frill or divided on the neck, their beauty of design is often very remarkable. But Cibber used the more normal type of cherub also, as well as being a master of the swag, the scroll, the hanging curtain, and other familiar accessories of the rococo style. To him too belongs apparently the credit of a much rarer and nobler form of cherub, that grand conception of a head with great curved wings framing a monument, such as Rysbrack later used upon the Reade tomb

[1] This notebook is more fully described in Chapter XI.

at Hatfield. It is one of the very rare cases in which
an angel type is invested with dignity in our sepulchral
sculpture, and stands out as an impressive and devotional creation in an enormous class of works which
is elsewhere only pretty at the best.

The cherub, as already said, is the emblem of immortality. He may be standing or sitting, an *amorino*
rather than a cherub, as in Henry VII's Chapel, or
flying, a full-length figure, as in the work of Cibber
and Bushnell ; or he may be the mere winged baby
head, beautiful or grotesque, familiar in the seventeenth
and eighteenth centuries, and surviving on village tombstones into the 1850's. Now he holds an attribute,
spade perhaps and reversed torch, emblems of labour
and rest, as on the Shakespeare monument by Gerard
Johnson and the tomb of the fifth Earl of Rutland at
Bottesford by Gerard's brother Nicholas (Plate II) ;
now a laurel wreath, as on that of the first Earl of
Hardwicke at Wimpole ; now a skull or hour-glass ;
now a flaming heart or urn ; now a palm branch,
common alike in Elizabethan and in Stuart days.
Anything appropriate seems in fact to have been
assigned to him, and the reader may find worse amuse-
ment than in making his own list of cherub types.

The hour-glass, which was part of the regular church
furniture of the sixteenth, seventeenth, and eighteenth
centuries, was a funeral symbol whose appropriateness
needs no emphasis. Winged and crowned, it marks the
work of Nicholas Johnson (Plate II ; p. 119), but is otherwise not very common on monuments of any preten-
sion, though frequently used in relief on the panels of
alabaster monuments and as an ornament on the cornice
of many good mural tablets, and on village tombstones
all over England. A good instance of its appearance
on an important later monument may be seen at Offley
on the tomb of William Chamber (*ob.* 1728), signed by
the almost unknown William Palmer.[1]

All these types and symbols were deeply rooted in

[1] Works by him may be seen at Wadhurst and at Horsted Keynes.

English minds as right and appropriate to " our pious forefathers," [1] and like the skull survived into the nineteenth century on village headstones long after they had disappeared from more ambitious works. The symbols derived from classical sculpture must next be considered, the sarcophagus, the urn, and the obelisk or pyramid, the use of which was one consequence of the intercourse of English with Italian sculptors when a strong Government has succeeded the chaos of the Wars of the Roses, and England had begun to play a part other than military in European affairs.

Henry VII, as we all know, brought Torrigiani and his fellows into England, and if the master's name was anglicised to Torrisany, we may be sure his inferior countrymen too had English nicknames, and, like John Guldo of Hereford (p. 13), settled in England; that Englishmen worked under him the records show. These men brought with them the *amorini* of their native land; they brought, too, the decorative use of wreaths and swags, the symbolism of the obelisk and pyramid, emblems of eternity, which, used at first in the round to adorn the cornice of the great architectural monuments also introduced from Italy, came by degrees to dominate the whole design, and finally to influence the arrangement of the figures themselves. The square altar-tomb of English tradition became a sarcophagus, nominally hiding the mortal remains of the dead actually interred in a vault below; and in the course of time this sarcophagus took on a more classical aspect. Either it was used alone; or with busts or allegorical figures placed on or about it; or with recumbent effigies, imitated from those of the great sarcophagi of the second century, often in Roman dress, upon the lid. [2] Or it might be flanked by figures of the Virtues, or the gods and

---

[1] This is stated in so many words by a writer in the *Connoisseur* in 1753.

[2] Plate XII.

goddesses befitting the character of the dead, Æscula-
pius and Hygeia for a doctor,[1] Minerva and Justice for
a statesman or a judge,[2] the Muses for a poet. The
sarcophagus itself may vary in shape from the plainest
of chests set upon lions' feet to the most elaborate
fluted forms reminiscent of those in use in Christian
times, and like them it may bear sculptured ornament.[3]

But the allegorical figure is not a growth of the
eighteenth century, as a familiar quotation should
long ago have shown us. " She sat like Patience on
a monument, Smiling at grief," is a phrase aimed not
at the courtier only but the groundling ; therefore in
Shakespeare's day the allegory was already an element
in monumental art, and if that allegory becomes steadily
more learned, it was a natural growth, embodying new
elements as time went on.

The urn is such another symbol. Originally used
in England as a mere decorative attribute, a convenient
centre-piece for a cornice if alone, or pairing well right
and left of an heraldic shield, it ascends in the seventeenth and eighteenth centuries to the dignity of a
centre-piece. Sometimes husband and wife will lean
upon it, sometimes a single allegorical figure will rest
sorrowfully against it, or—in the age of sentiment
initiated in literature by Sterne and echoed in sculpture as in painting—either wreathe it with flowers or
cling broken-hearted to this symbol of the dead. This
last development is obviously dangerous as paving the
way for the weak and ill-modelled figures in shapeless
draperies which disfigure so many nineteenth-century
tombs, and its great early practitioner, John Bacon,
R.A. (1740–99), cannot be acquitted of responsibility.
In earlier days a tomb of the more ambitious order
was at least designed for the individual ; when Bacon
standardised the Mourner and the Urn, his connection

---

[1] Plate XXX (a).   [2] Plate XI.
[3] The most interesting Italian sarcophagus in England is that wrought
by Benedetto da Rovezzano for Wolsey's never-completed tomb, and
used, nearly three centuries later, over the grave of Nelson at St. Paul's.

with Coade's artificial stone factory at Lambeth, with
its illustrated catalogues and endless replicas of approved
designs, was no inconsiderable factor in the downward
path.   Monuments of this type are found from Jamaica
to Devonshire, from London to North Wales, and,
pretty as they are, their repetition is a lamentable
thing.   Bacon too, I fear, is responsible for the Dying
Flower, which falls from the hands of several of his
symbolic figures,[1] as well as for those effigies of Faith,
Hope, and Charity whose baleful influence is still felt
in our churchyards ; the popularity of the broken
column, I regret to say, appears to date from Flaxman.[2]
But before going further into the history of our monumental imagery, we may devote a word to the lighted
lamp.

In its origin this too seems to have been classical.
It appears as an ornament on the cornice of many
seventeenth-century monuments, often with gilt flames
issuing from it ; it is sometimes carried by a cherub ;
but its frequency on the works of Bacon, the most devout
of Methodists, requires some Christian explanation
which one of his works provides.   At the feet of the.
graceful upward-gazing figure of Catherine Willett at
Great Canford—probably the sculptor's latest work,
since it is signed and dated 1799, and the sculptor died
in August of that year—is a lighted lamp.   She is one
of the Wise Virgins ; and the lighted lamp is therefore
the sign of Christian preparation, on Bacon's works
at least.

The crown of glory may be found, though rarely, in
eighteenth-century works such as the tomb of Sir
Robert Ladbroke at Reigate or on the remarkable
Spencer monument at Offley, probably by Stanton ;

[1] The cut rose appears on a monument at West Horsley signed by
Read, a pupil of Roubiliac, in 1767, but I think this is an isolated case
at the date, though it is used by Van Gelder twenty years later.
[2] He uses it on an otherwise beautiful Neo-Hellenic monument to
William Miles at Ledbury and elsewhere.   The sole earlier instance I
have met with is in an unidentified drawing by Rysbrack in the Victoria
and Albert Museum.

3

here and there, as on Gibbons's Mrs. Beaufoy or the
very similar Mrs. Kendal and Lady Grace Gethin,
also in the Abbey, a woman kneels as the heavens are
opened before her ; but as a rule the more elaborate
monument of the seventeenth and eighteenth centuries refers to the life or death of the subject, not to
the mysteries of faith. Of Bacon's share in the change
something has been said, and his short life—he was not
fifty-nine when he died—inspired his son, the still more
prolific John Bacon, Junior, to carry on with ever-
decreasing merit his stock designs of the Christian
virtues. But the most important works both of father
and son are above such trivialities, as Westminster
Abbey and St. Paul's will show ; and there is no stronger
proof of the strength of the old tradition of combining portrait and allegory than their works in those
churches. Allegory, be it observed, but not religion ;
the fear of Popery was still too strong in England. The
inscriptions, even on the most elaborate monuments
of the " pagan " eighteenth century, are frequently
as devout as they are obviously sincere ; yet Christian
imagery is almost unknown, cherubs apart—and they
are decorative rather than serious—until Roubiliac
about 1758 crowned the cenotaph of Edward Holds-
worth, the Commentator on Virgil, at Gopsall, Leicester-
shire, with a figure of Religion holding a cross and
pointing to the sky. Less than twenty years later
Robert Adam designed and Van Gelder executed the
monument at Warkton to a Duchess of Montagu on
which a life-sized angel consoles the mourners grouped
besides her urn [1] ; and in the next decade the figure
gazing upwards towards a heavenly light, or beholding
a vision of flying angels bearing the cross, makes its
appearance.[2] Here again Bacon was largely responsible,
and the surprising number of sketches he made for
the monument of John Romaine in St. Andrew's-by-

[1] Plate XXVI.
[2] Visions of heaven, symbolised by cherub heads in glory, are of earlier
date : Cibber, Stanton, Rose, and Rysbrack all make use of them.

the-Wardrobe are proof of the care he lavished on the subject. Yet, though this is one of the best works of its class, we have only to glance from the relief to the superb bust of Romaine himself to see in what direction the artist's strength lay.

The reason for this insistence on the classical idiom, and its sequel, the absence of Christian imagery—an absence which by no means excludes the most devout and Christian language in the epitaph—may be summed up in words already used : the fear of Popery. A quotation, more than thirty years after the beginnings of the Oxford Movement, will show how astonishingly recent is the now universal use of crosses as sepulchral emblems, and why they were shunned so long. In the text to Plate IX of the anonymous *Monumenta*, or designs for monuments ranging from elaborate altar-tombs to simple headstones, referred to in Chapter I, we read : " It is rather strange, to say the least, that those who object to a cross because it is, they say, ' Roman Catholic,' offer no objection whatever to urns, which are most decidedly pagan in their origin." This in 1867–8. Nor had the generation to which Faith, Hope, and Charity were so dear the right to throw stones at its predecessors' Wisdom, Fortitude, and Justice, figures every whit as abstract and as allegorical. Such imagery is not lacking even on the village tombstone. The pyramid may exist, though I have never seen it, for the Pyramid of Cestius was not within the ken of village masons ; the sarcophagus is very rare ; the urn excessively common, probably because it was at once easy to do and decorative in effect. In certain East Sussex churchyards, where pottery is still made in the district, the tombstone is decorated with inset urns or baskets of flowers made in terracotta, the chief artist, as appears from the specimens in the Sussex Archæological Society's Museum at Lewes, being one Jonathan Harmer. The urns are the symbol of death, the flowers of resurrection ; and when, as sometimes happens also on more imposing monuments, the urn is wreathed with flowers, both motives are combined. But common as the urn is, its symbolism was easily misunderstood. The Roman method of burial was unknown to the villager ; and when Mrs. Margaret Hunt of St. Ives, Huntingdon, died in 1787, the cherub on her tombstone removes the cover from an urn full of the skulls and crossbones familiar on a thousand headstones with the air of a *chef* displaying the contents of a large tureen. For such bathos we can only compare the filial piety which at South Mimms has given a beard to a fluttering cherub head, while retaining the childish outlines of the cheeks and hair ; yet the verve of that cherub displaying the contents of his urn, the carving of that bearded angel, would put to shame most of the marble angels, doves, and children in our churchyards to-day. These efforts of the village mason are among the very few tombstones which are frankly ludicrous, and the absurdity lies not in the types but in the misunderstanding of them. For urns and angel-heads were consecrated by long use, and love and grief are sacred in all ages.

CHAPTER III

COSTUME AND ITS CONVENTIONS

It is a commonplace that the mind of any age is reflected
in its monuments, and for a long period this is equally
true of its costume. Whether we are in search of
chain mail or plate armour, head-dresses with horns
or points, a citizen's dress or a King's robes, the monument is the best place in which to find it. Square toes
or pointed shoes, veils or coifs, helmets, whether practical
or heraldic, priests' vestments or ladies' broideries,
they are there, alike on the humbler brass or the royal
or noble monument on which all the arts of the marbler,
the founder, the coppersmith, and the gilder have been
lavished; and for the study of such things in detail
the reader may be commended to the originals, or to
Mr. F. H. Crossley's *English Monuments*.

No effort is required to appreciate their beauty, nor
that of the grand recumbent effigies or kneeling figures
of the sixteenth and early seventeenth centuries. We
have been trained to admire them, to see in them the
perfection of sepulchral sculpture; but 150 years ago
they were comparatively little noticed. Wesley found
the only Christian works in Westminster Abbey, " among
heaps of unmeaning stone and marble," not in the tombs
of Aymer de Valence or John of Eltham, but in Roubiliac's Nightingale and Hargrave monuments, which
to Dean Stanley were merely theatrical and grotesque.
Why does the modern guide-book to any church in
which monumental figures in Roman dress are found
abuse them without mercy, whereas eighteenth-century

critics found them noble and magnificent ?   To answer
these questions, it is necessary to understand something
of the history of monumental costume as distinct from
that of daily life.

For centuries indeed, the two are undistinguishable,
and monumental figures are costume pieces in the
fullest sense, as well as great works of art ; but there
comes a time when this costume, however realistic,
becomes conventional. The elaborate armour worn
by many early Tudor knights is certainly commoner
on their tombs than it was in real life ; so late as the
middle of the seventeenth century it may be studied
in detail on such works as the tombs of Sir Thomas
Lucy at Charlcote or Sir John Evelyn at Godstone
(pp. 128, 156).[1] But this applies to the statelier form
of monument ; on busts and kneeling figures the buff
coat and breastplate of actual warfare are far commoner,
and the Tower of London will suffice to show that when
the sculptor did represent armour, he represented the
armour, as he represented the civilian dress of the
day, with careful accuracy. Whether, therefore, we
would study the judge's coif, the soldier's cuirass, the
baby's frock, the Cavalier's love-locks, the widow's
hood, or the court lady's curls, we shall do so best upon
their tombs, because those tombs are in the round :
Vandyck and Holbein are here less useful.

Up to 1660, then, monumental costume is usually
that of official or of daily life. Exceptions there are :
a strange archaic Greek character belongs to Stone's
stone slab in honour of William Curle at Hatfield, and
the same sculptor's Holles monument in the Abbey,
based as it seems to be on Michael Angelo, prophesies
of many Romano-British warriors to come. The greater
dignitaries of Church and State continued to be repre-

---

[1] So late as the middle of the eighteenth century Roubiliac represented
Sir Thomas Hooke at Wootton St. Lawrence in full armour ; but this
was for archæological reasons, as he was clearly copying a contemporary
portrait. John Ashburnham's is the latest I know of the older recumbent
type: he died in 1673 ; one of the very latest monuments showing a *standing*
figure in full armour is that of Michael Richards (*ob.* 1721) at Old Charlton.

sented in their robes of office ; but their attitudes underwent a significant alteration. Now and again, as in the monument of Archbishop Lamplugh at York, we find a standing figure ; but for the most part the recumbent attitude is preserved, with a difference, till this in its turn became old-fashioned ; action superseded meditation, and by 1753 we find Lord Chief Justice Spencer-Cowper seated in the act of delivering judgment, attended by the figures of Justice and Prudence [1] ; in 1779, Chatham in the act of delivering a speech. But the robes remain constant, for the simple reason that the artistic possibilities of the costume appealed to the sculptor, who found in official robes as in the canonicals of the bishop—and the monumental use of the mitre in the later seventeenth century is far more frequent than the casual observer is apt to suppose (p. 45)—a suitable and even necessary distinction of dress. Not till Chantrey vested Lord Erskine in a toga do we find a lawyer's statue classicised.

Other classes of monuments followed another course. The fashion imported from France of combining a periwig and a Roman dress, or the more consistent method of representing the entire figure *à la romaine*, became almost universal in the case of monarchs and military commanders, and held sway for nearly two centuries. Civilians during the reign of Charles II were, however, usually represented as in life, and the fashion continued, in their statues commonly, in their busts almost universally, until the Regency, when a little drapery became the sole garment of two busts out of three. But the toga and the close-cut head govern our official sculpture, with honourable exceptions at all times, for a century and a half, expiring with Gibson's Peel in Westminster Abbey, which he is said to have refused to execute unless the use of Roman dress were permitted him.

It may be worth while to expand what has been said, so far as the costume of post-mediæval monuments is

[1] Plate XI.

concerned, mediæval monuments themselves being, as
we have seen, rigidly realistic in this point.

The men on early Tudor tombs are clean-shaven
and distinguished by hair cut straight across the fore-
head and on the neck, the women by caps and veils ;
then the veil becomes an appendage, or its place is
taken by a coif or by a cap with a small frill beneath
it. A great lady will wear a jewelled coif, a great noble
the robes of the Garter,[1] but armour is the most usual
form of male costume, unless for priests or lawyers.
Monuments of the reign of Henry VIII are not too
common, and few are more satisfactory than the charming tomb of Sir Richard Shirley of Wiston (ob. 1549),
a work possibly of the Sussex artist mentioned on
p. 25. He stands in armour bareheaded, his helmet
resting on a rock beside him, a wife on either side.
His eyes look up to Heaven, his hands are raised in
prayer ; the ladies in coifs and veils, with heavy gowns
and hanging sleeves, stand right and left in profile,
also praying. It would be hard to find a more perfect
example of the costume of the period, so strangely
petrified for us upon our playing-cards ; but the especial
interest of the work is the bold and early transition to
the standing attitude, the admirable pierced base, with
its three quatrefoils flanked by trefoil-headed openings
and the delightful scroll work which frames and flutters
between the three figures.

But the work is only part of what it was. The figure
of the Dove once hovering over Sir Richard Shirley,
which connected it with the remarkable group of
Sussex monuments elsewhere described, is gone, gone
too the brackets which once supported figures of two
saints. In all England indeed it would be hard to find
monuments more maltreated than those at Wiston.
The once stately tomb of Sir Thomas Shirley, father of
the famous Shirley brothers, is reduced to two figures

---

[1] *E.g.* on the monument of the first Earl and Countess of Rutland at
Bottesford (*Art Journal*, 1903, p. 272). The children round the altar-tomb
are admirable examples of early Tudor costume.

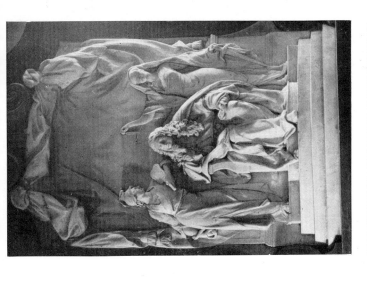

MONUMENT TO LORD CHIEF JUSTICE SPENCER COWPER, HARTINGFORDBURY. BY L. F. ROUBILIAC, SHOWING THE TRIUMPH OF REALISM COMBINED WITH THE ALLEGORICAL ELEMENT IN THE ATTENDANT FIGURES.

PLATE XI.

MONUMENT OF RICHARD SACKVILLE, WITHYHAM. BY C. G. CIBBER, SHOWING THE TRADITIONAL ELEMENTS OF AN ALTAR TOMB WITH WEEPERS MODIFIED BY THE MORE DRAMATIC TENDENCIES OF THE DAY. (P. 55.)

PLATE X.

facing p. 40.

MONUMENT OF SIR ISAAC NEWTON, WESTMINSTER ABBEY.
BY J. M. RYSBRACK. A TYPICAL WORK OF THE PERIOD,
WITH RECUMBENT EFFIGY IN CLASSICAL DRESS, PYRA-
MIDAL BACKGROUND, ALLEGORICAL FIGURES AND RELIEF
ON THE SARCOPHAGUS.

PLATE XII.

facing p. 41.

placed upon a window-sill; but the fragment of Sir
Richard's remains supremely interesting, alike as an
example of costume and composition.

With the reign of Elizabeth we come also to the
reign of the farthingale, a Spanish fashion introduced
into England soon after the middle of the sixteenth
century and inordinately popular for the next fifty years.
The cap continues to be worn under the hood, and a
cloak frequently hangs from the shoulders. Brocades
are indicated not by diaper work, as in the Middle
Ages, but by elaborate patterns in relief. The men
wear armour or doublet and hose, or in the case of
divines and lawyers official robes, and the ruff is always
present, though it ranges from the modest frill to the
most elaborate structure of wired lace or lawn. The
plain falling collar of linen appears over doublet and
armour before the end of the century, but on the whole
the costume of the age is curiously constant. One great
change indeed there is : the monument ceases to be
confined to the man of rank, and spreads to the middle
classes, who had hitherto been content with slabs or
brasses when they had a monument at all.[1] But they
did not aspire to recumbent effigies : the new fashion
of small kneeling figures suited both their purses and
their aspirations, and such figures of merchants and
their ladies, the latter sometimes wearing hats, become
very frequent.

Nor do the early years of James I show much variation. The mural tablet and the bust come into general
use ; the allegorical figures and finials on the great
canopies grow more elaborate ; but the dresses remain
of the same type, the bodice, open or high-collared,
and the farthingale and ruff for the women, elaborate
armour, trunk hose, or official dress for the men. Even
the cap which we associate with Mary, Queen of Scots,

[1] The brass indeed died hard ; examples of marble altar-tombs and
surrounds with portraits inlaid in brass under a canopy are very frequent
between 1560 and 1600, survived in Wales till the end of the seventeenth
century, and at St. Mary Cray actually till 1749.

like the little frill inside the collar of the dress, goes on
into the 1620's, the great standing ruff from 1580 or
thereabouts to 1630. It is therefore hard to date
an Elizabethan or early Jacobean monument from
dress alone : the effort fortunately is rarely necessary.[1]
The hair both of men and women undergoes little
change between 1560 and 1610 ; men wear it cut short,
with the beard made fashionable by Henry VIII in his
later years, now broad like his, now pointed, at the
discretion of the wearer ; the women wear clusters of
curls about the ears, but the cap or hood is far commoner
than the high dressing of the hair favoured by Queen
Elizabeth. About 1610 the example of Henry, Prince
of Wales, led to men's hair being worn long and brushed
back over the head,[2] that of Anne of Denmark to the
dressing of women's front locks over a high frame often
adorned with flowers or rosettes, a fashion frequently
represented on monuments. The ruff develops into
an enormous lace collar, standing out nearly a foot
from the very low-cut gowns of the day ; where a close
gown is worn, the large ruff is its usual accompaniment.[3]
Less common is the enormous hood, like the eighteenth-
century calash, worn over the close-fitting cap or coif ;
good examples are to be seen at Leyton, Elmley Castle,
and Narborough, and an interesting variation with the
hood elaborately fluted occurs at times, as in a fine
work at Henley-on-Thames.

But the Vandyck dress proper casts its shadow
before, both for men and women, and the costume
familiar in Mytens's portrait of Charles I at the National
Portrait Gallery occurs on many monuments. The
high falling collar, the trunk-hose softened from the
grotesque exaggeration of their earlier form and shaped

[1] The reader will find the series of effigies in the Ancient Monuments
Commission's volume on Westminster Abbey instructive on the point.

[2] An excellent example is the D'Arcy monument at Hengrave, mentioned
in the last chapter.

[3] Examples, by the same hand, I think, are the Lady Lucie Stanley,
née Percy, at Walthamstow, and the Elizabeth, Lady Montagu at Chid-
dingly. Both suggest the school of Johnson in its later development.

to show the knee, the doublet cut in a peak in front
and tied with elaborate points, the high boots and
slashed sleeves, may be found on many monuments,
the grandest perhaps that of Sir Giles Savage at
Elmley Castle (Plate XVIII).   About 1635 the Vandyck dress itself makes its appearance.   There is
an exquisite example at Hillingdon, with the most
charming family group, father, mother, and two little
girls, it is possible to conceive (Plate XVII) ; the low
short-waisted bodies edged with lace and the soft
falling skirt free from the tyranny of the farthingale
can hardly be better studied, though the clusters of
curls about the ears are more elaborated in such works as
the Evelyn monument at Godstone or the lovely Lady
Savage at Elmley Castle.   Among men the kneeling
figures on the Hertford tomb at Salisbury are true
Vandycks in marble, noble alike in conception and in
execution ; it is characteristic of the age of Herrick
and Sir Thomas Browne that these admirable portraits
and the shrouded figures breathing of the charnel-house
should appear side by side in our churches.

The Civil War put an end to monumental sculpture
on a large scale, and when effigies do appear under the
Commonwealth, as at Wimborne, the dress is usually
severely plain : the ladies wear close hoods, the
men gowns or armour or plain doublets and collars[1] ;
they carry on, that is, the tradition of the past,
though here and there such a work as Fanelli's Mrs.
Delves (*ob.* 1654) at Horsham suggests the Vandyck
charm.

Now and again a definitely transitional monument
will occur, like that of Colonel Popham (*ob.* 1651)
and his wife in Westminster Abbey.   Popham was a
Puritan, and it is all the more significant, as showing
the pressure of the new tendencies in art, that he
and his wife are represented standing, he in armour,

---

[1] Apparent exceptions to this plainness of apparel such as Lord Cottington's effigy in Westminster Abbey will usually be found to have been
erected in the lifetime of the subject.

she in loose classic robes, to right and left of the
great urn on which they lean ; but for his costume,
the work might have been signed by Rysbrack in the
1740's.[1]

With the Restoration these new tendencies are more
fully developed. Charles II was four times and James
II twice represented as a Cæsar by Gibbons alone[2] ;
that sculptor's huge tomb of Viscount Campden shows
him and his wife in Roman dress[3] ; but monumental
art is conservative, and it took long for the traditional
recumbent effigy in contemporary costume to be altogether ousted. Bushnell and Cibber, the leading
sculptors of the reign of Charles II—for Gibbons's work
was primarily decorative, and his monuments are
relatively few—exemplify both tendencies. Each
worked in both manners, though Bushnell naturally
tended to the Roman and Cibber to the realistic, as their
respective works on the Royal Exchange sufficiently
show[4] ; but each could work well in either, as Cibber's
Romanising monuments at Bottesford[5] and Bushnell's
in contemporary dress at Chirk and Great Billing are
enough to prove. The little church of Ashburnham,
with its two remarkable monuments executed within five
or six years of one another, the one a belated instance
of the stiff effigy in plate armour, the other a dramatic
scene of parting (p. 55), is an epitome of the conflicting
forces at work on English sculpture ; but the classical
had it easily, helped as it was by the literary fashions
of the age, and Stone's Holles monuments in the Abbey,

[1] Popham's was the only monument of a Commonwealth worthy to
be left in the Abbey after the Restoration. The inscription was defaced,
and the work moved from Henry VII's Chapel to St. John's, and there
re-erected, in deference to the feelings of his brother, a member of the
Parliament which had accepted the return of Charles II.

[2] At Windsor, Chelsea Hospital, Edinburgh, and the Royal Exchange.
One James II is at the Admiralty ; another, at Newcastle, was melted
down in 1688 and re-cast for the bells of All Saints'.

[3] Reproduced in the *Architect*, October 1921, from the plate in the
Rutland Magazine, vol. iii, No. 23, Front.

[4] See *The Times*, May 24, 1925, December 3, 1926.

[5] *Art Journal*, 1903, p. 275.

like le Sueur's bust of Charles I as a Cæsar,[1] are prophetic of much that was to come.

One significant echo of the Golden Age of English divinity is the return to the use of the mitre, and even the cope, on certain episcopal and archiepiscopal monuments. From 1631 to 1688 at least eight examples exist, and one isolated instance, due to special circumstances probably, is found as late as 1714 ; a list may not be without interest, as showing the remarkable character of this return to the earlier ceremonial practice of the Church.

1. Archbishop Harsnett, *ob.* 1631. Chigwell. The most remarkable seventeenth-century brass in existence, showing the Archbishop vested in cope and mitre.[2]

2. Bishop Creyghton, *ob.* 1672. Wells. Recumbent effigy wearing mitre.

3. Archbishop Sheldon, *ob.* 1674. Croydon. Recumbent effigy, the work of Latham and Bonne in 1676, originally very fine but greatly damaged by the fire of 1879.[3]

4. Archbishop Sharp, *ob.* 1679. St. Andrew's. Recumbent effigy, with an angel exchanging a mitre for a martyr's crown. This might be taken as purely symbolical but for contemporary analogies.

5. Archbishop Sterne, *ob.* 1673. York. Recumbent effigy wearing mitre, probably the work of Cibber.

6. Bishop Gunning, *ob.* 1685. Ely. Recumbent effigy wearing mitre, strongly resembling the Sheldon (No. 3).

7. Archbishop Dolben, *ob.* 1686. York. Recumbent effigy, perhaps the work of Latham.

8. Archbishop Lamplugh, *ob.* 1688. York. Standing effigy wearing mitre, probably the work of Cibber, to whose statue of William of Wykeham at Winchester it bears a strong resemblance. One of the most impressive monuments of the age.

---

[1] Mentioned by Walpole, but still unpublished.

[2] Strictly speaking, brasses are outside the scope of this volume, but the work could hardly be omitted from a paragraph on ecclesiastical dress.

[3] Finely engraved in Lysons, vol. i, p. 183. Notes on the work in the Vertue MSS., 23071, fol. 42*b* ; 23073, fol. 55*b*.

9. Archbishop Sharpe, *ob*. 1714. York. Semi-recumbent effigy wearing mitre. A very late and interesting example, the costume influenced perhaps by the usage of the Province and the monuments of the two preceding Archbishops, Sterne and Dolben. This may well be the work of André Carpentier.

All are realistic, and easily appreciated; their classicised contemporaries need more explanation. If the Englishman *à la romaine* perplexes us to-day the Englishman *à la romaine* in a curled periwig does so still more. Yet the age " dressed the image of our Saviour over the altar " at Nuremberg in 1716 " in a fair full-bottomed wig very well powdered " [1]; and if in lay sculpture that " odd mixture of an old beau, who has a mind to be a hero, with a bushel of curled hair on his head and a truncheon in his hand," seemed grotesque to Lady Mary,[2] it seems even more so to us, to whom the " fair full-bottomed wig " is not, as it was to her, a matter of everyday experience. The Romanising costumes of Grinling Gibbons had at least the merit of congruity ; the hair was short and the head laureate in the most approved Augustan fashion, to correspond with the cuirass, cloak, and greaves. The addition of a realistic wig plays so large a part in the sculpture of the first half of the eighteenth century that we must accept it as a convention and not dismiss as contemptible the art in which it is employed ; to do so we must first consider the sister arts of painting and of literature. For it was the Age of Allegory, and it is only when we do not study Verrio or Thornhill or the minor poets of Dodsley and the *Dunciad* that we fail to grasp that sepulchral art was bound to follow its fellow arts. Allegories on ceilings and staircases fall into their place in fitting buildings, or are readily ignored by the passer-by ; poets slumber forgotten on the shelf ; monumental sculpture is insistent and conspicuous, a contrast often to its surroundings, and

---

[1] *Letters of Lady Mary Wortley Montagu*, August 22, 1716.
[2] The same, September 28, 1718.

because we do not understand its idiom we condemn it offhand. How many Londoners have ever heard of the Apotheosis of Thomas Guy ?   It is to be seen in Guy's Hospital,[1] and is one of the strongest proofs of Thornhill's decorative powers ; and if the founder of a hospital could be received into Olympus on a ceiling, why should not Prior be attended by the Muses on his monument in Westminster Abbey ?   How many readers of Pope even—and they are a class elect and precious—understand that when Pope told King George that his

> Word is Truth, as sacred and rever'd
> As Heav'n's own Oracles from Altars heard,

he was using, satirically perhaps, language which was moderation itself compared to that employed by other poets as by the artists of the time ? [2]

Sculpture, like other arts, must express itself in the terms of its own age, and when poets and painters united in classicising their great men, sculptors were bound to do the same in what we may call official sculpture. And even this official sculpture has its merits. The head may wear a periwig or the Augustan laurel ; the dress may be that of an *imperator* as understood by the Renaissance ; but as portraits these works are always admirable, far better—let us say it honestly—than the average bust of a Greek philosopher or Roman emperor. They were careful studies from the living model, or, if posthumous, from the portrait or the death-mask, and not mere copies of other copies, as our surviving ancient portraits so often are ; and when this vivid portrait art is combined, as sometimes happens, with contemporary dress or undress, it is, once our eyes are opened to see the man under the

---

[1] For the first time reproduced in November 1926 in *Drawing and Design* as an illustration to my short article on English Baroque.

[2] There is a familiar print of the Apotheosis of Two Children of George III ; and if the reader of to-day has forgotten Southey's poem on that monarch's death, Byron's " Vision of Judgment " is remembered.

wig or nightcap, wholly delightful. The art to which
such things belong was a living art, ready to adopt
an accessory from any source, no doubt, and not always
consistent in symbolism, setting, or costume ; but it
was true to the post-mediæval tradition of resolute
portraiture. Idealism had no place in the features of
the deceased ; the sculptor's business was, first and
foremost, to get a good likeness ; and the extraordinary
number of masks from the dead and from the living
catalogued in sculptors' sales during the eighteenth
century is a proof of the trouble taken. The setting
was a secondary matter, depending often less upon
the artist than the patron, as we can see from the way
in which Cibber's gruesome fantasies were discarded
when his monuments came to be executed.

It is rash to generalise on insufficient evidence, but the
key to this use of classical costume would seem to
be supplied by two great monuments, that to the third
Duke of Ancaster (*ob*. 1763) at Edenham, the work
of a sculptor unknown to the historians, Charles Harris,
and that to the Earl of Fauconberg (*ob*. 1700) and his
son at Coxwold. The Duke is seated in peer's robes,
his son, dead before him, stands by in classical costume ;
the Earl stands in the normal dress of the day, with
periwig and square-cut coat, holding a coronet in his
hand, his son, dead over fifty years before him, wears
Roman armour and stands beside him in a dramatic posture. Why this difference, unless the Roman
dress connoted death ? The contrast is evidently
intentional, and, taken with the habitual use of that
costume for statues of kings, generals, and other great
men, is highly suggestive. The duke and earl appear
as in life ; to indicate their sons' premature deaths
those sons are classicised : therefore, it would seem,
classical costume implies heroisation. This clue explains
much that is perplexing in our sculpture, much that
to the uninitiated appears grotesque : Roman dress
is the outward and visible form of immortality. Great
ladies, too, may wear it as early as the middle of the

seventeenth century,[1] but it is never so widespread as for men. The medallion portraits of women found on many eighteenth-century works give us in delicate relief the equivalent from the hands of Rysbrack or Roubiliac of portraits by Hogarth and Allan Ramsay. A rose in the hair or at the bosom, pearls round the neck, a modest lace tucker, a loose curl falling on the shoulder—such things have a charm of their own in an age when the hair was more simply dressed than it has been before or since. Where a medallion portrait of a man occurs, it is usually wigless and realistic. Was this because it was often founded upon a death-mask, whereas the lady's was based upon a portrait? Certainty is impossible, but the instinct to portray a woman at her best is deeply rooted. Nor must the wig itself in all its forms lack due commemoration, the rather that its effects are there when it is absent. For the nightcap—a misnomer, since it was worn in the day as easy deshabille—was the wig's corollary. So hot a headdress required a substitute when it was re-moved, especially since, as we know from Corporal Trim's remarks when Uncle Toby was courting, the head was often shaved. And if the cap of every day was preferred to the more pompous wig [2] by the man or woman who desired to erect a monument, it is hard to blame them for choosing the familiar and domestic aspect of a dear one.

Sculpture, as already said, possesses the immense advantage of being in the round; now and again the fact leads to surprising discoveries. Most of us, it is probably true to say, conceive of the Lely wig as curly behind as before. So it is; but with the Kneller wig, whose cascades of curls frame the face so impressively,

---

[1] *Cf.* Mrs. Popham in the Abbey (p. 43) and Cibber's monument to the eighth Earl and Countess of Rutland at Bottesford.

[2] It is surely an odd point that, while Bolingbroke offended the homely Queen Anne by appearing in her presence in a tie-wig instead of a full-dress one, Louis XIV the ceremonious should have presented the English Ambassador Matthew Prior with his own bust in a nightcap. The bust is now in Westminster Abbey.

the case is altered. " The gentlemen stay but to comb,
ma'am," was the excuse for delay in appearance in
the drawing-room,[1] but the wig they combed was a
front only, as the statue of Sir Robert Clayton at
St. Thomas's Hospital, erected in 1714, shows. Those
impressive locks were worn over the lank natural hair,
which is combed behind the ears and tied on the neck
—the rudiments of a tie-wig, in fact, only that the tail
was natural.[2] It was but a matter of a few short years
for the flowing curls themselves to vanish, and to be
replaced first by a shorter, curlier wig, then by a regular
tie, such as we see in Roubiliac's bust of Garrick in the
National Portrait Gallery. Then the curls at the sides
grow few—compare Nollekens's Charles James Fox of
1793 in the same room with that same Garrick of five-
and-thirty years before ; then short hair comes in, in
Fox himself as a symbol of his sympathy with Brutus
and the French Revolution, in the soberer part of the
world with Mr. Pitt's tax on powder, as the Antiquary's
Caxon found to his cost ; and we are in the age of Chantrey and the Prince Regent's curls, that transition to
our modern world. Only bishops retained the wig, old-
fashioned prelates right down to the 1850's[3]—a wig
little changed from that we see in episcopal portraits
at Lambeth a century before.

One odd freak of the tie-wig deserves to be chronicled,
since it was not only carried to excess by the Macaronis
of the 1770's, with their enormous masses of hair
behind tied with flowing ribbons, but was actually
worn by serious people. J. F. Moore's statue of Beckford
in the Guildhall is so high up that the vast bunch of
hair behind does not attract attention, but a cast of
the head seen in a private collection proved that the
huge and clumsy mass of the pictorial satirists was there

---

[1] Congreve.

[2] This is presumably the case with that on his splendid statue at Bletchingley, but it is impossible to see that work from behind. See p. 105.

[3] My father, born in 1840, was confirmed by Bishop Vowler in 1856,
and was deeply impressed by the prelatical wig, the last, he was told, of
its kind in England.

on the neck, little as it might be suspected from the
modest and misleading front with its smooth parting
and close rows of little waves.

So, too, with portraits of women. Sculpture gives
us the side and back views which are lacking in the
paintings, and just as the ringlets of Henrietta Maria's
Court,[1] the looser Lely curls,[2] the more elaborate piled-up
tour or *fontanges* of the Kneller age [3] are well represented on monuments, so the closely brushed-back locks
of the Hogarth portrait are to be found. The dress
may be of the age, a laced bodice, a loose wrapper, a
widow's hood ; or it may be frankly classical, though
this is comparatively rare ; what we do not find in
sculpture is the immense piled-up head-dress of the
next or Fanny Burney period. Sculpture simplifies,
and even where the hair is dressed high, as in Rysbrack's Queen Caroline at Windsor and Hertford House,
or Bacon's Queen Charlotte, executed in commemoration
of the famous visit to Whitbread's Brewery at which
Peter Pindar made mock, nothing exaggerated appears ;
a hint of fashion was enough.

Once at least we may meet with a soft muslin cap
or turban, on Banks's justly celebrated Penelope
Boothby (p. 84), and here it seems to befit the childish
simplicity of the rest. We must look to the painters
and the satirists, to Romney, Reynolds, Sayers, and
Rowlandson, to realise the extravagance of the coiffure
of the age.

When we come to the Regency, Nollekens's busts
and such monuments as Flaxman's Lady Fitzharris at
Christchurch faithfully reflect the hairdressing of the
day, that of the Jane Austen heroine, with hair piled
high behind and short curls framing the face. Here
again the front view is better than the profile, and the

---

[1] There are several examples in Stone's work ; a lovely later instance
is the statue of Thomasine, Lady Evelyn, at Godstone (p. 156).

[2] Bushnell and Cibber are the sculptors in whose work this phase is
best represented.

[3] Gibbons and Bird use it fairly frequently, Cibber in its earliest development in his Dame Dorothy Brownlowe at Sutton.

effect from behind—an effect impossible to gauge except in the round—is positively ugly, disguising as it does the shape of the head and dragging the hair upwards instead of downwards ; nor is the look of the short locks with a wreath of curls on top worn by the contemporary man so good in sculpture as in Lawrence's paintings, as any of Chantrey's countless busts of the Prince Regent will show.   And the unfortunate habit—universal almost from 1790 to 1860—of merely covering the shoulders with scanty drapery instead of grappling with, and overcoming, the difficulties of contemporary dress, renders a collection of busts of the age as depressing as a row of Roman copies of Greek philosophers, at the Capitoline Museum.   It may not be irrelevant to conclude with a riddle which must date from that eighteenth century in which its subject played so large a part, a century in which the Portuguese dressed up a figure of Christ in a long wig when they carried it in procession through the streets of Rome.[1]   " What is perfect with a head, perfect without a head, perfect with a tail, perfect without a tail, perfect with either, or neither, or both ? "   Answer : A wig.

[1] *Letters from a Young Painter to his Friends in England*, 1750, i, p. 214; *cf.* the Nuremberg story on p. 461.

CHAPTER IV

THE GROWTH OF REALISM

Upon their Backs the ancient Statues lie,
Devoutly fix'd with Hands up lifted high,
Intreating Pray'rs of all the Passers-by.
At length they chang'd the Posture by degrees,
And plac'd the Marble Vot'ry on its Knees.
Their Warriors rough devoutly Heav'n adore,
And Statesmen kneel who never knelt before.
Next a less pious Posture they provide,
On Cushions lolling, stretch'd with careless Pride ;
With wringing Hands the little Cherubs moan,
And Fun'ral Lamps appear to blaze in Stone,
And Marble Urns with juster Beauty stand,
And rich Relievo shows the Master's Hand,
On the neat Altar with a Busto grac'd,
In *Roman* Pride, like that which *Sheffyld* plac'd.[1]

From the Poem prefixed to Dart's *Westminster Abbey*, 1723.

THE mediæval effigy is invariably recumbent, with hands joined in prayer or crossed upon the breast, and clad in the dress of his age and calling. The attendant figures, if any, are saints, angels, monks, or children according to his state of life ; the character of his monument depended on the purse and taste of himself or his successors. Now the tomb will be of the simplest—the son of the Conqueror has a plain wooden effigy at Gloucester—now it will be adorned with all the arts of marbler, enameller, or metal worker. The setting may be the plainest of altar-tombs, or it may be a shrine enriched with carved canopy and grille of bronze or Sussex iron. One thing all such effigies have in common, the recumbent attitude which symbolises

[1] This alludes to the bust of Dryden, then recently erected in the Abbey.

death [1] ; yet at the very time when this emphasis on death led, as we have seen, to the emphasising of death's most ghastly aspect, the cadaver, we have the first hint of the reverse process. The figure comes to life, in prayer still, it is true, but still in a posture possible only to the living. The father of the Lady Margaret takes his wife's hand upon their tomb at Wimborne, removing his gauntlet to do so ; and the same church—Tewkesbury—which contains one of the latest instances of the rotting body gives us, in the fourteenth century, the kneeling figure of Lord le Despencer placed in the canopy above his tomb. By the time Prior Wakeman's cadaver was in place, six years or more after the Dissolution of the Monasteries, the kneeling suppliant has become tolerably familiar ; and, like the latest of the recumbent figures, he has also become a portrait. Henry VII desired in his will that his effigy, kneeling in prayer, should be placed above the shrine of Edward the Confessor, though his own glorious tomb by Torrigiani preserves the older pose. The movement was slow, for sepulchral art is essentially conservative ; but the reign of the " lolling " figure, as Dart calls it in his poem on Westminster Abbey (1723), part of which is prefixed to this chapter, had begun long before the effigy in the old sense—the figure recumbent as if lying in state, and often coloured to the life—had passed out of use, and the figure seated, standing, or reclining on the elbow had taken its place. [2]

An example or two will illustrate the point. As early as 1626 Nicholas Stone had represented young Francis Holles as a Roman soldier (p. 44) ; fifty years later the Loyal Duke of Newcastle and his learned Duchess, side by side in the Abbey, lie as they would have lain four hundred years before. The same surprising contrast may be found elsewhere. The gallant

[1] To the very few mediæval effigies which Mr. Crossley will allow to be portraits, I would myself add the exquisite priest at Brimpton, holding a chalice to his breast. He is said to have died while administering the Sacrament to his flock during the Black Death, and the face is so personal that a portrait must, I think, be intended.   [2] Plates IX, XI, XII, XXI.

Cavalier, John Ashburnham, lies stiffly, one of the latest of our effigies clad in full armour, between his wives upon his tomb at Ashburnham, their sons and daughters kneeling on a panel below in the approved tradition ; his brother's monument is one of the most striking examples of the new spirit brought into English sculpture at the Restoration. This second monument, by Bushnell, and Cibber's Dorset tomb at Withyham, are unique in their age for their emotional quality, as the first is unique in its complete emancipation from any traditional sepulchral form. It is nothing that William Ashburnham wears pseudo-Roman dress and periwig as he kneels with hands held out to detain his dying wife, whose spirit is with the flying angel placing the crown of immortality upon her head ; his face of passionate grief, his agonising gesture, are alone remembered. So too with the gay and witty Dorset, who kneels beside his dying son, his wife upon the other side ; the frozen grief upon his face awes us to silence, and it is only with an effort that we can fix our minds upon the style, and realise that this is an extension of the mediæval idea of the altar-tomb, and that, though the mourners have become the principal figures, their other children, dead and living, carved upon the sides of the tomb on which their brother lies, are in the old tradition still (Plate X).

These works bring us face to face with a new world of art. We may call them, as Walpole called the Nightingale monument, more theatric than sepulchral ; but they are personal, passionate, and express in sculpture what before was spoken in the epitaph, the love and grief of the survivors.

When such things were done in England—and it is less odd than it seems that the Danish Cibber should here keep closer to the English manner than the purely English Bushnell, because Cibber, though he worked in Rome, was foreman to John Stone, whereas Bushnell, by bent and later training, was wholly of the Rome of Bernini—it is not surprising to find the older type of effigy on the verge of extinction, and even the kneeling figure rare.

Nor was the impulse towards movement confined to England. There are few more significant stories than that which records that Richelieu's niece Madame d'Aiguillon, discussing the Cardinal's monument, told Bernini that his Eminence had always intended to have himself represented in the act of offering himself to God and not in the act of prayer [1]—in action, that is, not in repose. Henceforth the typical effigy stands, sits, or "lolls," indifferently, and the impulse towards movement—even in the modified recumbent figure which is what Dart means by that ungracious phrase— grows ever stronger (Plate XIII).

Before the death of Charles II, Clement Spelman (Plate IX) was standing in his Recorder's gown above his grave; thirty years later Bird seats his learned Dr. Grabe upon his own sarcophagus in Poets' Corner; and a whole series of judicial effigies, from Green's Judge Powell (*ob.* 1713) at Gloucester to Flaxman's Lord Mansfield in the Abbey, attests the national sense that great lawyers should appear alive, not dead.

The altar-tomb itself varies with the centuries. Saints and weepers give place to children, ranging from warriors in plate armour to babes in swaddling bands; Gothic tracery to the niches of a Roman sarcophagus resting on classical pillars, or to columns separating the panels, plain, twisted, or carved into the semblance of a tablet leg, bulbous or adorned with carved angular panels; or it may still be plain on two or three sides, and adorned on the side or at head and foot with an heraldic shield or coat-of-arms, often in a richer marble and magnificent in design.

As with the tomb proper, so also with its surroundings. The growth of the architectural setting is another marked feature of post-Renaissance sculpture. The shrine or canopy of mediæval days might be architectural in the fullest sense; but in such cases the

---

[1] A. Michel, *Histoire de l'Art*, vi, ii, p. 727.

element of prayer for the dead was so frequently involved that when, after the Reformation, the monument
became a memorial pure and simple, a type of setting
came into existence to fit the new conditions. Hence
the canopy of Tudor and Jacobean days, sometimes
a mere hint of an arch, oftener an elaborate tester
resting upon two or four pillars, Doric or Ionic being
often combined with Corinthian on the same work, with
a ceiling, usually arched and deeply enriched with
coffering, beneath which, as under a canopy of state,
the statues of the dead stand, sit, or recline at the whim
of sculptor or of patron. So familiar was the convention that Dryden even uses it as an illustration of
the art of Congreve :

> Fine Doric pillars found your solid base,
> The fair Corinthian crowns the higher space.[1]

Sometimes the framework took on, from Elizabethan
days, that is, a new shape, the tent door with looped-
back curtains, which may become a canopy of state
or a mere frame enclosing the inscription, often with
cherub heads to hold it back.

Whatever the setting, the figures below fall into two
main types, that with recumbent effigies, often leaning
on the elbow, and that in which the dead man and
his wife kneel on either side of a prayer-desk. These
last are very numerous, very much of a kind, and we
may well ask what evidence there is to show that they
were not, like mediæval monuments, ordered wholesale from the sculptor. There is one complete and
satisfactory answer—the figures at least must have
been made to individual order, because children, as a
rule, form an integral part of the design. In the case
of mediæval tombs, accessory figures could be, and
doubtless were, added as required to a ready-made
altar-tomb; where a monument required the children
to be shown, any wholesale preliminary carving was

[1] " To my dear Friend Mr. Congreve, on his Comedy of the Double
Dealer."

impossible. The families of the age were enormous,
and no sculptor could possibly tell beforehand how
many daughters would be required to kneel behind or
below the mother, how many sons symmetrically to
attend their father ; and the principal figures at least
were usually portraits. There is, as already said, no
more striking proof of the prosperity of England under
Elizabeth than the wide diffusion not of magnificent
monuments only, but of less costly works. Merchants
and lesser country gentlemen, who in mediæval times
would have been contented with a brass, now employed
a tomb-maker, often, as stylistic details show, the same
who executes the monuments of great knights and nobles,
just as in later Stuart days they demanded monumental
tablets from the sculptors employed on tombs more
splendid, the same materials being used for both.

But these kneeling figures, these often-repeated
compositions with their alabaster panels and rich
coffered settings, and dark marbles such as touch to
set off the more translucent materials, go gradually
out of fashion.[1] They belong to the old tradition, and
a newer art is in the air. The figure leaning on its
elbow sits more upright, the varieties of pose become
more numerous, the accessories tend to the classic
swag or the rococo shell, and these, though at first
combined with such emblems as the skull and crossbones, the hour-glass and scythe, finally oust the latter
altogether from all but the humbler types of monument.

Caroline sculpture indeed, even when the great
names of Le Sueur and Fanelli are taken into account,
stands in the main upon the old ways, but reflects
the new tendencies at times. A scholar, Stow, Dean
Boyce of Canterbury or Sir Thomas Lucy of Charlcote,
grandson of Justice Shallow, may sit or lie among his
books ; a warrior may appear in Roman dress ; re-

[1] The latest use of the scheme is perhaps the tomb of John Abel, the
architect-builder of Herefordshire, at Sarnesfield (*ob*. 1674), made by
himself when over ninety years of age and showing himself and his two
wives kneeling.

cumbent effigies of the old type meet us everywhere ;
kneeling figures, both of parents and children, abound ;
busts, whether bronze or marble, become yet more
common ; portraits in relief are occasionally found.
The allegorical figures conspicuous on the Salisbury
monument at Hatfield are yet more emphasised in
such a work as Stone's monument to Lady Digges at
Chilham, where the portrait has altogether disappeared.
Stone's work indeed is an epitome of the contending
styles of the age ; but sculpture, like every art save
that of the pamphleteer, received a sudden check in
1642, because monuments were looked upon as sinful,
Popish, and idolatrous by the more extreme members
of the Puritan party. There is more than the evidence
of such devastation as was wrought at Peterborough,
Lichfield, and Lincoln, to bear witness of the fact. In
the little church of Marholme, some seven miles from
Peterborough, is the bust of a little boy with long
curls framing a gentle face ; below it is his name, and
an address "To the courteous Souldier," without
parallel, so far as I know, in our epigraphy :

> Noe crucifixe you see, noe Frightfull Brand
> Of superstitions here, Pray let mee stand.
> Grassante bello civili.

It was in vain ; the child's nose is broken, and the
break is centuries old.

And such vandalism was deliberate. If Tom Hearne,
that sturdy Jacobite, declares that at St. Helen's,
Abingdon, "old monuments have been defaced and
unduly destroyed by Puritans, Presbyterians, and the
rest of the whining crew, purely out of a vain, idle
conceit, that the memory of no Roman Catholicks ought
to be preserved"[1] ; the judicial Hobbes can be cited
to prove that his words are no exaggeration. In that
section of the *Leviathan* that deals with the Kingdom of

---

[1] Quoted in Miss L. Toulmin Smith's *Leland*, v, p. 115. Weever's
Funerall Monuments abounds in descriptions of the hatred of the earlier
Puritans for what they looked on as " remaines of Antichrist, papisticall
and damnable."

Darkness he finds it necessary to explain that " monuments of friends, or of men worthy of remembrance,"
are not " against the second commandment," " for such
use of an Image is not worship of the image ; but a
civil honouring of the person, not that is, but that was."
Thomas Dingley again, whose MS. *History in Monuments* (c. 1680), facsimiled by the Camden Society in
1866–7, is one of the most valuable records we possess,
repudiates " the sordid opinion in some people that
Tombs and Monuments, with epitaphs, relish of Romish
Superstition and Popery." We need ask no stronger
testimony to the power of Puritanism to see evil where
no evil was. Reaction of course was inevitable. Monuments grew ever more elaborate, the portraits on them
more alive. Only the Protestant scruples of successive
Deans and Bishops kept St. Paul's bare of monuments
till 1795, long after Reynolds had publicly lamented
the overcrowded state of Westminster Abbey, and had
urged the erection of future monuments in the Cathedral.
The delay was disastrous in more ways than one, chiefly
perhaps because the great age of portrait monuments
was past when St. Paul's was at length opened to
receive visible memorials of the dead ; but it had
not the smallest effect on the development of English
monumental sculpture, which till the age of Neo-
Hellenism maintained and expanded that tradition of
resolute portraiture which, as Hogarth said of painting,
was the consequence of " religion, the great promoter
of [the historical] style in other countries, rejecting it
in England."

Mediæval art was static, devotional, generalised in
type though exquisitely minute and accurate in details
of costume ; and it may be said to have expired in the
cadaver of Bishop Bushe at Bristol (1558) and the
tomb of Geoffrey Chaucer (1556), beside which a priest
could say mass. The Renaissance sets in, and the
effigy, so long recumbent, comes to life first kneeling,
then reclining, then sitting or standing as taste dictates.
The accessory figures, originally still and in the act

of prayer, partake of this dynamic movement. The emphasis—save in that school of the charnel-house of which much has been said—has shifted from death to life, though skull and crossbones, urn and sarcophagus precede the weeping willow of our grandfathers as symbols of mortality. Allegory gathers round the grave ; history plays her part upon it ; religious imagery, cherubs apart, is notably absent. But the portrait grows in realism from masterpiece to masterpiece ; sepulchral art becomes steadily more personal, more closely linked with the dead man himself or with some scene in his past life. The classical and the baroque combine with English tradition to form a style mixed indeed, but generally admirable in technique, and always excellent where portrait art is concerned. But the time was at hand when unstinted abuse was to take the place of praise equally unstinted, and the protagonists of the new movement were Sir Joshua Reynolds, Thomas Banks, and John Flaxman.

CHAPTER V

NEO-HELLENISM AND THE GOTHIC REVIVAL

WE have seen how the mixed style of the eighteenth century was evolved, and how, while varying elements entered into the composition of English monuments, the resolute verisimilitude of the English portrait was never lost sight of in the process of development. There was nowhere a conscious break with the past, a deliberate passing from one stage to another. But a change was at hand. The travels of "Athenian" Stuart and of Robert Adam had their effect on the monuments which both were called upon to design less in the general form of the work than in the delicate classical detail which began to make its appearance ; and 1764 saw the publication of Winckelmann's epoch-making *History of Ancient Art*.

The excavations at Herculaneum in the 1750's created an immense amount of interest all over Europe, and the science of classical archæology was founded when Winckelmann had set himself to write the history of Greek art in the light of ancient authors and modern discoveries. His services to the serious study of the subject cannot be over-estimated, but his conclusions were seriously vitiated by two facts, neither of which he could know, and as those conclusions were taken as gospel by the artists of his own and the next generation, they had certain unfortunate results. These two facts are that almost all the works on which he based his conclusions were not Greek originals at all, but copies, often not even at second hand, of lost originals, of no more stylistic value than those which fill the Via

Babuino to-day ; and that the technique of these copies, when, as often happens, the originals were in bronze, might be highly misleading. Nor did he take into account what he could and should have realised, that the restorations habitually inflicted on them from the fifteenth to the eighteenth centuries are more misleading still.

But Winckelmann preached a new gospel, the supremacy of Greek art and the necessity of getting back to Greek principles : and Europe listened and rejoiced. His teaching was reinforced by Lessing, and its influence on monumental art may be seen from Sweden to Malta : the Renaissance was for the time dethroned. His was a great idea, that of working out the contribution of the Greek spirit to the history of art ; but his materials were lamentably imperfect, and the subsequent use of ancient art as a touchstone by which to try, and to find wanting, all later developments was a grave error. The cry " Back to Greece " was in fact responsible for that total breach with traditional art known as Neo-Hellenism.[1]

Rome had always been, as she always will be, the centre of artistic inspiration ; but the sculptor who went there after Winckelmann went with a new purpose. The works of Michael Angelo, John of Bologna, and Bernini had played no small part in the education of his predecessors. We know that Stone, Cibber, Bird, Rysbrack, and Scheemaker copied their works as well as those of the ancients ; that Roubiliac possessed casts of Bernini's Apollo and Daphne ; and that when, in 1758, the Duke of Richmond threw open a Gallery of Casts for the use of budding sculptors in London itself, the masterpieces of the Renaissance were to be found side by side with the Niobe and Laocoon, whether thanks to the Duke or to the Gallery's Keeper, Joseph

---

[1] The universal character of this breach with the past can be admirably seen in Muet's *History of the Knights of St. John of Jerusalem* (1827), where mediæval, Renaissance, and Neo-Hellenic art appear in succession in this single and limited field.

Wilton, just home from making his name in Florence, is immaterial. But after Winckelmann the Renaissance was out of favour, and men like Banks and Flaxman went to Rome in the fixed belief that the secret of sculpture lay in ancient art alone.

Reynolds, though a personal friend of Roubiliac, was deeply interested by this new and congenial doctrine of the Ideal and Typical in sculpture. To criticise it does not even seem to have occurred to him, and he carried it to extreme lengths in his Academy teaching. In the Tenth Discourse he laid down a new commandment, the devastating doctrine that the patron " who wishes not to obstruct the artist, and prevent his exhibiting his abilities to their greatest advantage, will certainly not desire a modern dress," since the use of that dress in sculpture involves " prostituting a great art to mean purposes." And he had both the will and the power to enforce his doctrine. When the Jamaican Assembly asked the Royal Academy to choose a sculptor to execute a monument to Lord Rodney, Bacon, whose design was selected, produced a beautiful model, shown in the Fine Arts section at Wembley in 1924, representing Rodney in the naval uniform of the day, a sailor of King George's navy. The sculptor was successful, but he was forced to modify his design, and in his statue at Spanish Town Rodney is apparelled as a Roman general. Again, when Bacon was selected to execute the statue of Dr. Johnson for St. Paul's, family tradition avers that the Doctor was to have worn the wig and coat which we all know, and that Reynolds forbade it, using his position as Chairman of the Committee which had undertaken the matter to insist on his friend's appearing in the garb of a Greek philosopher, a dress which, in his opinion, would have improved the statues of the Apostles in St. Peter's. Johnson himself knew better. "A man," said he, as J. T. Smith records, " for ease may wear a nightcap in his own chamber, he ought not to look like one who had taken physic in his portrait ! " What would he have said had he known

MONUMENT OF DR. BUSBY, WESTMINSTER ABBEY. BY
FRANCIS BIRD. PROBABLY THE FINEST SEMI-RECUMBENT
FIGURE OF THE AGE.

Plate XIII.

facing p. 64.

PRIMATE STUART, ARMAGH, BY SIR F.
CHANTREY, SHOWING ATTIC FORMS PERFECT-
LY COMBINED WITH MODERN REALISM. (p. 78.)

PLATE XV.

facing p. 65.

MRS. PETRIE, LEWISHAM, BY THOMAS BANKS,
R.A. SHOWING CHRISTIAN BELIEFS TREATED
IN THE TERMS OF ATTIC *STELAE.* (p. 65.)

PLATE XIV.

that his own intimate friend insisted on his being represented in St. Paul's as if he had just had a bath ?

When Reynolds denounced " the desire of transmitting to posterity the shape of modern dress " as a sacrifice " of everything that is valuable in art " he was only carrying out Winckelmann's principle of the Ideal and Typical ; but when the President of the Royal Academy laid down such a law, when he counted it his mission to " counteract the evil effects of so powerful an example " as Bernini's, when Flaxman both in his papers in the *Artist* and his Academy Lectures denounced the mixed style of the Renaissance as degenerate and worthless, young sculptors naturally shrank from representing the one or studying the other. Their training became lop-sided, the eye, taught to consider one form of art alone legitimate, ceased to take pleasure in anything unclassical.

Two important works, little more than thirty years apart, may illustrate the point. When Roubiliac commemorated the Duchess of Montagu in 1753 by representing the Three Fates at their appointed work,[1] he was expressing the sorrow of the survivors in terms of pagan mythology, as contemporary critics were not slow to point out, though those terms had become part of the consciousness of the civilised world.   When Banks designed his great relief of the death of Mrs. Petrie,[1] he set Faith, Hope, and Charity beside her dying bed.   But Banks's Christian Virtues are infinitely more classical than Roubiliac's Fates—as Greek as Mrs. Petrie's couch and lamp, or the youthful ephebe weeping at her feet : the contrast is the measure of the change wrought by Winckelmann's teaching upon the art of Europe.[2]

Equally significant are the enormous funeral vases of Attic type erected by Sir Roger Newdigate at Harefield, Middlesex, in memory of his mother and his

[1] Plate XVI.   The same figures, only completely Hellenised, were used by Schadow and in Wimborne St. Giles as at Berlin.   The same church contains Rysbrack's monument of the first Earl of Shaftesbury, with a noble bust taken as Walpole tells us, from Cooper's miniature.

[2] Plate XIV.   At Lewisham.

wives. The two first are by Richard Hayward, a minor sculptor of the 1770's and 80's, the third by the younger Bacon. The earliest is adorned with a representation of a classical figure reclining on a classic couch and partaking of the Banquet of Immortality ; the next bears a figure of Faith copied line for line from an archaistic Aphrodite on a candelabrum in the Vatican. Both are so unlike Hayward's usual urns and vaguely classical female mourners that we can only ascribe them to the taste of the Hellenist Sir Roger himself, who prepared the blackened niches on the S. wall of the chancel for their reception.

Nor is the Christianised third, to Sir Roger's second wife, less notable. Bacon, that most devout of Evangelicals, forced to use a classic form, substituted for the pagan figures of his predecessor a figure of Religion holding up her hands in ecstasy to an angel vision.

The Clapham School, indeed, to antedate a convenient term, protested strongly against the " heathen allegories " of the time, from the use of Etruscan vases on the altar-piece of old St. Mary Abbot's, Kensington, to the appearance of the three Fates at Warkton. The subject of a monument had in fact become a matter of conscience with the strict at the very moment, strangely enough, when the Protestant scruples of successive Bishops of London had been overcome, and St. Paul's was being filled with the largest possible works in the worst possible manner, that of an acquired code, not a tradition evolved, as previous styles had been, out of the artistic experience of successive centuries. Examples of Neo-Hellenism in its earlier and purer form will serve to show how deeply it had penetrated the artistic conscience of the leaders of the movement. Banks executed a portrait of Princess Sophia of Gloucester as Psyche, a group representing Mrs. Johnes of Hafod and her infant daughter as Thetis and Achilles ; and in modelling the busts of Warren Hastings and Horne Tooke " for love of their noble looks " he " meditated upon Plutarch's heroes." Flaxman, when called

on to design a monument to Professor Sibthorp in
Bath Abbey, showed that eminent botanist, robed in
the briefest possible himation, with Hermes's travelling
hat atop, stepping off a boat, having finished the
voyage of life, and hastening towards a Greek temple with
a bunch of flowers in his hand.   Sibthorp travelled
in Greece, and ultimately died of consumption there
contracted.   Bath, where he settled upon his return,
must have been aghast at the spectacle presented
by a contemporary translated in so strange a fashion.

Yet the work is in itself a beautiful design.   Flaxman's training with Wedgwood had developed his
perception of the value of the silhouette, and much of
his monumental work is essentially outline, modelled
on the minor Greek art of vase painting as much as
his designs for Homer themselves.   Its purity of decorative detail is most attractive, and where he con-
trives to give something of a Greek effect without
ignoring contemporary dress, as in his monument to
Dr. Warton at Winchester, the result is an example
of that intelligent combination of different artistic
elements to which we owe so much of our finest monumental art.[1]   But this is not pure Neo-Hellenism.
Winckelmann might never have been born for all we
see of him in Banks's admitted masterpieces, the Penelope
Boothby at Ashbourne and Speaker Chute at the Vyne,
Hampshire, whose terracotta models at the Soane
Museum and the Victoria and Albert Museum will
show their quality if the originals are inaccessible ; as
for Flaxman's great figure of Lord Mansfield in the
Abbey, it so dominates the Hellenisms at its base
that they are utterly forgotten, and the same sculptor's
statue of Sir Robert Ladbroke at Spitalfields, were
the surface more freshly carved, might have been signed
by Roubiliac himself.   The reason is not far to seek.
To represent a Lord Chancellor or Lord Mayor otherwise
than in official robes were to throw away the advantages
of a dress at once sculptural and typical, and Flaxman

[1] *Cf.* Plate XV.

knew it ; works such as these are therefore in the direct line of our great sepulchral art.

Of the sculptors of the next generation those most strongly affected by Neo-Hellenism are E. H. Baily and John Gibson, the former chiefly before his R.A. days. Redgrave, it is true, states that Baily's art " did not derive its inspirations from any classic source "; but in such works as those at Egham the influence of Flaxman's studio, in which he worked as a youth, is overwhelming ; the monument to Hannah Gostling might, like its companion by Flaxman, have been composed under the instructions of Winckelmann himself, and is completely in keeping with the Greek character of the whole church (p. 104). Gibson's later Hellenisms, diluted with Victorian prudery, abound in the Diploma Gallery ; his great early works at St. Nicholas, Liverpool, commissioned no doubt through the influence of his patron Roscoe, are in a very different category. Both are to members of the Earle family, both are grandly conceived and nobly executed, without a trace of that sugariness which pervades his later work. The grand Eros of the one, the splendid Hellenic Justice of the other, may rank with the finest allegorical figures in our art.

Flaxman's desire to Christianise sculpture, a rather later development, was helped by the religious reaction against Neo-Hellenism already referred to, a reaction, however, equally hostile to the tradition prevalent in England before Winckelmann. Monumental art is conservative, and the Gothic Revival took longer to affect our sculpture than our buildings ; but when Banks acquired the Gothic figures removed from the old Guildhall Chapel from Alderman Boydell, when Flaxman took to executing Gothic monuments such as we may see at Salisbury,[1] still more when, as we find from the catalogues of Coade's Artificial Stone Factory, Gothic monuments, fonts, screens, and pulpits could

---

[1] Blake's passion for Gothic may well have influenced Flaxman in this later phase of his art.

be ordered from stock designs, the way was clear for the Gothic Revival as applied not to architecture only but to monumental sculpture. The Oxford Movement gave a religious sanction to what was in fact one aspect of the Romantic Movement, and its leaders failed to realise the unwisdom of a complete breach with tradition, to perceive that Gothic art adopted *en bloc* and on principle was bound to fail as Neo-Hellenism failed before it, and as any movement must fail which consists in adopting wholesale the conventions of an earlier period.

The belief that Gothic is essentially the Christian art may seem an odd one in an age which aimed at returning to the first six centuries ; but the explanation is simple. Later Renaissance art—the art, that is, of the seventeenth and eighteenth centuries—savoured of the Latitudinarianism which the new leaders of the Church detested ; its monuments therefore passed under the same condemnation, and there was an ever-growing desire to return to the convention of the mediæval tomb. From 1840 onwards figures of Deans and Bishops recumbent under Gothic canopies abound, and when Ruskin lent the weight of his authority to the movement the fate of the art he denounced was a sorry one. For sixty years seventeenth- and eighteenth-century tombs were removed or mutilated without scruple even in the Abbey itself ; those that were left were denounced or ridiculed ; and it is only in the twentieth century, with such figures as the standing Bishop Creighton in St. Paul's or the kneeling Archbishop Temple at Canterbury, that signs of a revolt against the mediæval convention in our conservative ecclesiastical tombs have become apparent.

Minor Gothic works, such as the deplorable tablet to Charles and Mary Lamb at Edmonton, erected in the 80's, show more clearly than any words the futility of a style based on imitation only ; yet when the Gothic Revival set in, the neo-classic tradition was outworn. Literature had freed itself from classical trammels by finding a style of its own, and not by imitation of

earlier forms ; it is the misfortune of English sculpture
that twice over it fell back upon the distant past, the
Greek first and then the Gothic, and took over its
formulas as canons of taste. Imitation, not creation,
was therefore its keynote ; there is no Wordsworth in
its annals ; and it was reserved for Alfred Stevens,
in the face of doubt and discouragement, to insist upon
the contribution of the Renaissance to sculpture, and
to link his work with a tradition unbroken till the rise
of Neo-Hellenism.

An admirable protest against the action of those
inspired by the Gothic Revival in their merciless
treatment of " those monuments of past generations
which are valuable chiefly as memorials of persons and
families, and which are found guilty of defacing or
obscuring the beauty of architectural features, or which
interfere with modern arrangements for reseating
churches, or with those for warming them " is given by
J. G. Nichols as editor of Dingley's *History from Marble*
already alluded to (vol. i, p. 18). The examples which
he gives could unfortunately be multiplied a hundred-
fold, and as he specifies the Temple Church as one of
the worst examples of this wholesale clearance, it may
be added that one of the finest of the displaced monuments, that of John Hiccocks (*ob.* 1726), is rapidly
perishing in the churchyard from the effects of weather,
and has lost its background within the last year or
two.

No chapter on Neo-Hellenism can afford to ignore
the work of John Deare, though he alone among
our sculptors is not recorded to have made a monument.
His excellent training in Carter's workshop, his rivalries
with men of the established reputation of Eckstein
and Van Gelder, his joy at the praise of Reynolds when
he got the Academy gold medal, his delight when John
Bacon, R.A., applied to him for his services, his going
dinnerless to see a Shakespeare play, are recorded for
us in the pages of J. T. Smith, largely in the form of
extracts from the young sculptor's own letters. He

visits Sir Horace Mann ; arrives in Rome fortified with
introductions from Reynolds ; carves a Marine Venus
for Sir Richard Worsley,[1] a Judgment of Jupiter and
an Eleanor and Edward for Sir Corbet Corbet, of which
more anon ; obtains £470 worth of work for Granville
Penn,[2] executes chimney-pieces for the Prince of Wales
and Lord Bristol ; copies the Apollo and the Venus
dei Medici for Lord Berwick ; makes busts of Prince
Augustus Frederick, Lady Webster, Mme. Martinville,
and " one of the Dickensons," as well as small reliefs
for the second-named lady ; and copies the Ariadne
for Mr. La Touche. He died suddenly in the arms of
the brother of Grignon the engraver, from a chill caught
by sleeping on a peculiar block of marble to gain inspiration for the figure which he hoped to carve from
it, an eccentricity quite in keeping with the belief
that he must always pray naked.

All this is common property ; what has not yet been
done is to illustrate from his work his application of
the principles of Neo-Hellenism. Where his subjects
were classical, a classical treatment was appropriate ;
nor can we regret that the lovely bust of his patron
Penn in the Library at Eton was based on the Antinous.
If the Gray of the National Portrait Gallery is not
Hellenised—and as we hear of no other sculptor employed
by Penn, for whom it was made, it is almost certainly
Deare's work [3]—it is because its subject was thoroughly
unclassical in his outlines.

It is with the Edward and Eleanor, the original model
for which, with a relief of Hercules and Antæus
by the same sculptor, is in the Walker Art Gallery at
Liverpool, that we can really judge of the extremes
to which Neo-Hellenism could go. The English king
appears in the guise of a Pheidian Eros, seated almost

[1] At Appuldurcomb.
[2] Including the Landing of Julius Cæsar at Stoke Poges.
[3] I am responsible for the identification of the sculptor. The bust,
we know, was made from authentic materials for Penn, whose one desire
was a good portrait of his friend Gray, and would almost certainly be
made by the one sculptor whom Penn is known to have patronised.

naked upon a Greek couch, with a Greek matron of the fifth century B.C., Queen Eleanor to wit, bending to suck the poison from his arm. At the foot of the couch an amphora stands upon a tripod, and a veiled attendant, his back to the main group, buries his face in his hands. Against the couch leans a Greek shield, emblazoned with the lions of England.[1]

Refined and delicate as the work is, it is impossible to conceive a style less appropriate to its subject; herein, of course, lies its significance. When the principles of Reynolds and Winckelmann could thus be applied to a scene from mediæval history, the fatal nature of their theory becomes apparent, and accounts for much that is regrettable in nineteenth-century sculpture.

[1] Deare received £100 or £120 for the marble, unless a replica, as Mr. Whitten thinks, is involved by the two prices given. The model was exhibited at the Royal Academy in 1788.

CHAPTER VI

THE PENINSULAR SCHOOL

I VENTURE to coin this title for a group of sculptors whose best-known works are the monuments of the Peninsular heroes in St. Paul's Cathedral, such men as the younger Bacon, Manning, Rossi and Gahagan, Westmacott, Hopper, Baily, and Theed. But before we speak very briefly of them, we may note how quickly their work became out of date. *Vanity Fair*, as we all know, was published in 1847-8, and in it Thackeray speaks of their productions as " braggart heathen allegories " ; we may profitably compare Prince Hoare's boast in 1803 : " The vote passed in 1789 by the House of Commons, for the erection of sepulchral monuments to those who had died in the defence of their country, although it did not primarily spring from a regard for the Arts, afforded to the sculptors a happy opportunity of doing honour to themselves and to England. The monuments erected in the two cathedrals of the Metropolis, to the memory of various officers of our Navy and Army, will stand as records of the sudden elevation of sculpture at the present period." Alas for the instability of human taste ! " Braggart heathen allegories " they were in 1847, and are to this day; and it is not hard to understand the reason. They are badly designed and badly carved, the want of modelling being disguised by excessive polish ; they are the strangest mixture of Greek and modern, without the excuse that the Greek element corresponded, as did the Romanisings of a century before, with anything in the national consciousness. It is inconceivable that any revolution of taste can bring them again into favour, for even in their own day they expressed professional formulæ, not the spirit of the age. They are at once trivial and colossal, and in their swaggering emptiness we see the nemesis of Neo-Hellenism.[1]

Some of the sculptors were, it is true, capable of better things. *John Charles Felix Rossi* (1762–1839), an associate of Bacon's at the Coade Factory of Artificial Stone, went to Rome, became an R.A. young, and received a number of important commissions, notably from his patron Lord Egremont. He plays some part in the Farington Diary, and his art in his work in St. Paul's is less deplorable than that of some of his colleagues. His Captains Mosse and Riou (Campbell's " gallant good Riou ") in St. Paul's is a poor affair, a sarcophagus with medallions of Fame and Victory ; his Cornwallis is large but insignificant, though better than Flaxman's Howe, and his statue of Lord Heathfield in regimentals and military cloak is very fair, but for the dreadful pedestal, with a meanly carved Victory handing a laurel crown to a Greek soldier guarded by a preposterously big shield. His Rodney, also in uniform, might, however, be almost unreservedly praised but for the poor quality of the attendant Fame and Victory.

Sir Richard Westmacott (1775–1856) had a long and distinguished career. The son of a sculptor of the same name, the brother (?) of another (Henry), and the father of a third (Richard), he was responsible for the monuments of Pitt and Fox, Spencer Perceval and Addison in the Abbey, and for several works in St. Paul's, notably the monuments of Sir Isaac Brock, who sinks naked into the arms of an officer under the eyes of a deplorable Red Indian, and of Generals Pakenham and Gibbs, very fair statues in uniform. Westmacott's angels, feminine but attractive, can be seen at Ledbury and Malpas ; his Achilles, his Duke of York on the Column, and the pediment of the British Museum are

[1] Banks's efforts in the same field are dealt with on pp. 150–1.

familiar if not attractive, and the enchanting baroque children at the foot of the Bedford statue in Russell Square deserve to be better known. Not one of them, however, will compare in quality with an early monument or two at Gresford, near Wrexham, or with his fine scene from the Book of Job on his monument to Lord Pembroke at Wilton, which has a touching and beautiful quality curiously lacking in his national monuments. Both he and his son of the same name, sculptor of the fine recumbent effigy of the third Lord Hardwick at Wimpole, as Professors of Sculpture at the Royal Academy, preached the gospel of Neo-Hellenism to their hearers, and as late as 1871 students were taught to abhor Bernini and the Renaissance, and to aim at the Ideal and the Typical. As before, they responded; their response makes the work of Alfred Stevens a portent in the reign of Queen Victoria.[1]

It cannot be said that the younger Bacon (1777–1859) does himself justice in St. Paul's, though there is fine modelling and no glaring absurdity in his Sir John Moore, and his monument to Generals Craufurd and Mackinnon has at least shape and balance. But his earlier monument to Captains Harvey and Hutt, very badly placed against a window of Westminster Abbey, is really beautiful, though it only consists of two allegorical figures flanking an urn. The carving is good, the figures lovely, with that French dignity and distinction which Sir Edmund Gosse has noted in the latest works of his father the R.A., and for a man some years under thirty the work is very remarkable, more so than the similar efforts of a very much more famous man, Chantrey.

Bacon's pupil Charles, son of *Manning* (d. 1847), a sculptor whose work degenerated into bathos, executed the really fine monument to Captain Hardinge,

<hr>

[1] I speak of Sir Richard being the brother of a sculptor. Henry Westmacott will not be found in the handbooks, but I have seen two very competent works by him whose dates suggest that he was a brother of Sir Richard's. He may, however, have been a cousin, nephew of the first Richard Westmacott, whose sale catalogue of 1783 I have seen.

one of the few in St. Paul's which is not puerile or grotesque. Like the even finer memorial to the Rev. Isaac Saunders in St. Andrew's-by-the-Wardrobe, it bears the impress of the school of Bacon, and the mourning figures are as good as the sarcophagus is well proportioned.

E. H. Baily again, who lived till 1867, though he became an A.R.A. fifty years before, we have met in his early Hellenic stage, when his work was incomparably better than his famous Eve at the Fountain would suggest. In his ambitious monument to Sir William Ponsonby in St. Paul's, however, he was merely carrying out the design of another man, the elder *William Theed* (1764–1817), who, like Flaxman, worked both for Wedgwood and for the goldsmiths Rundell and Bridge. The result of their joint labour is one of the largest monuments in St. Paul's, which has been described as " a confused idea, wrought with a heavy hand." Ponsonby's horse foundered at Waterloo, and he was killed ; hence the enormous charger of Elgin Marbles type, minus all harness, against which the huddled body of Ponsonby lies naked, sword in hand, as he feebly stretches up to receive a crown of laurel from a Victory whose draperies are studied from the maidens of the Erechtheum. The whole thing is a tragic waste of labour, at once ungraceful and undignified, but it is only too typical of its period.

Gahagan, S. (fl. 1780–1820), the miserably paid assistant of Nollekens, won some popularity with his bust of Nelson, and his monument to Sir Thomas Picton, bad as it is, at least has a little more attempt at composition than some of those of his contemporaries. A bust of the Admiral stands on a pedestal guarded by a British Lion, while Valour and Genius stand on the left to receive a crown of laurel from a Victory on the right. The parts at least hold together, even if the execution is poor, and it is noticeable that the design is distinctly more Roman than Greek, as one might have expected from a pupil of Nollekens ; nor did Nollekens himself

execute a more delightful bust than Gahagan's portrait
of the younger Dr. Charles Burney on his tomb at
Deptford.

Henry Hopper (1803–1834) was responsible for the
monument to General Hay in St. Paul's, representing
him in his regimentals, sinking into the arms of a
colossal naked figure, a mourning comrade at his side
and three of his men marching into action on the field.
But for his unexplained and needless presence, we
might have felt some pleasure in the work, which, if
not inspired, is at least an honest attempt to represent
a contemporary battle-scene ; but that naked athlete
spoils it all, and as he is the largest and most insistent
feature of the work, we must regretfully dismiss it as
grotesque. Hopper's less ambitious tablets and mural
monuments are distinctly more successful, and may be
found all over England.

Even worse is the monument by *Kendrick* (*fl.* 1813–
29) to Sir William Myers, who died at Albuera, with
Wisdom and Valour shaking hands before his tomb,
which is surmounted by a bust. His less ambitious
works in Waltham Abbey and in Hammersmith Parish
Church are better ; like his greater fellows, the chance
of working on a large scale seems to have paralysed
both his invention and his execution, and we can only
regret that such opportunities were given to men so
little capable of using them.

It is refreshing to turn to the art of *Sir Francis
Chantrey* (1781–1842). Not that it was always good,
for it was not ; not that he was above the habit of
making his models and getting his assistants to carve
them [1] ; but that he had a real respect for the art of
his predecessors, and studied the work of very different
men with high enthusiasm. His Duchess of York at
Weybridge, his Vernon monument at Hanbury, are based
on Greek *stelae*, and are really beautiful ; whenever

---

[1] I have been assured by one who had it from a workman who was
on Chantrey's staff for over thirty years that Chantrey was an admirable
modeller, but left the carrying-out of his designs in marble to his " ghosts."

he went to Worcester he would spend hours in the study of Roubiliac's monument to Bishop Hough ; and if much of his official work is tame and indeed poor, many of his monuments—not, alas! those in St. Paul's— are very graceful and even powerful,[1] and his statues and some of his portrait busts, especially that of Sir Walter Scott, and of the writing-master Tomkins at the British Museum, are delightful. He admired Thorwaldsen, and knew Canova well [2]—and the younger men influenced his art not wholly for its good ; but the sculpture of the first half of the nineteenth century would lose much of its interest were Chantrey's best work to disappear. From 1806 to 1841 he is the most important figure in our sculpture ; and though we may regret that the dying pseudo-classic tradition gave us George IV in Trafalgar Square and on the Steyne at Brighton, the Pitt in Hanover Square and the Horner in Westminster Abbey, we must set against them the Cyril Jackson of Christ Church, the Primate Stuart at Armagh (Plate XV), the Bishop Shute Barrington at Durham, and the delightful Sir Joseph Banks at the Natural History Museum, and be grateful that there is so much to praise in an age of mediocrity.

[1] The tragic face of Johnes of Hafod, gazing on his dying daughter in the great group at Hafod, is a masterpiece, altogether finer than the better-known Pike-Watts monument at Ilam.

[2] Canova's colossal monument at Belton is one of the most important tombs by a foreign sculptor in England.

CHAPTER VII

IMAGINES INNOCENTIUM

THE child in mediæval sculpture is not individualised; nor could he be so when the effigies of kings and nobles were typical, not realistic. By the middle of the sixteenth century, however, the more important child-figures had become personal, and portrait art was the richer for the fact.

There are two quite distinct classes of children on our monuments—the dead to whom the tomb is erected or whose shrouded images attend their parents, the living who appear as mourners for their kin; the former class is by far the better known, and includes some famous works of art; the latter includes accessory figures only, but these are often of singular beauty and interest.[1]

Not that, where immense families are represented, these minor effigies are all of them portraits. When Grinling Gibbons, for instance, was called on to design the monument of Baptist Noel, third Viscount Campden, and set his family in low relief on the enormous structure, the eighteen children are palpably not treated with the care bestowed on the full-length statues of the parents. But portraits exist nevertheless—the exquisite figure of the heiress Elizabeth, Baroness Roos, on the tomb of the third Earl and Countess of Rutland at Bottesford would deserve attention at any period,[2] as would the brothers and sisters on the Elmley Castle monu-

---

[1] The little kneeling figure of Sir John Denham, the future poet, on his mother's monument at Egham, now sadly defaced, is one of the few cases outside royal and noble families in which famous men are represented in their youth. Mr. Frederick Turner informs me that this figure was removed when the church was rebuilt, found at a local shop, and restored by Flaxman.

[2] *Art Journal*, 1903, p. 292.

ment (p. 43); there is a delightful kneeling boy, Sir
Robert Cecil, on the Burghley tomb in Westminster
Abbey [1]; and a notable little daughter with plump
childish face upon the Shrewsbury monument (1617–18)
there.[2]   Stone has given us several kneeling children,
notably the Villiers group upon the Duke of Buckingham's tomb [3]; and there is something peculiarly
personal in the pretty children by their mother's deathbed on the monument to Jane, Lady Crewe (*ob.* 1639),[4]
one of the most touching, and least known, monuments
in the whole Abbey.

Such examples could be continued indefinitely;
before we mention others, it may be well to lay
down one or two general rules.   If the child is
alive at the parent's death, and introduced as an
accessory, then on mediæval or early Tudor monuments he is standing, in later works almost always
kneeling.   If such a child, whether kneeling or standing,
holds a skull, or has a skull beside him, then he too is
dead (Plate XX).   A swaddled babe—ghastly rows of
them, five and even seven at a time, may be seen on certain
monuments—is almost always dead, whether laid on
the ground at the mother's feet or in her arms; laid
in a cradle on a parent's tomb, he may sometimes
indicate the birth of an heir, as at Narborough, where
Clement Spelman as a baby lies opposite his own sepulchral statue; more often he is one more unfortunate
victim of the health rules of the age.   The dress of all
children, infants apart, is down to the end of the seventeenth century that of a miniature adult, save that the
lace-edged cap is worn by little girls and boys alike.
Where clothes are stiff and formal, the effect is sometimes almost ludicrous; but at times—and this is
especially true of the Vandyck dress worn by a little
girl—the result is charming.[5]   The little daughters of

[1] A. M. C., *Westminster Abbey*, pl. 128.   [2] *Ibid.*, pl. 141.
[3] *Ibid.*, pl. 128.   [4] *Ibid.*, p. 346.
[5] The stiffer dress of a slightly earlier period can be very attractive,
as in the kneeling girls on the Elmley Castle monument, with their fringed
sashes tied behind over close-fitting bodices.

MONUMENT OF MARY, SECOND DUCHESS OF
MONTAGU, WARKTON. BY L. F. ROUBILIAC. SHOW-
ING PAGAN MYTHOLOGY TREATED IN THE TERMS
OF CONTEMPORARY ART.

PLATE XVI.

facing p. 80.

THE CARR MONUMENT, HILLINGDON. ONE OF THE FINEST EXAM-
PLES OF THE LATER SCHOOL OF ALABASTER WORKERS, SHOWING A
NEW AND PERFECT UNDERSTANDING OF THE BEAUTY OF CHILDREN.

PLATE XVII.

facing p. 81.

Sir Edward Carr (*ob.* 1636) at Hillingdon, near Ux-
bridge, already noted, the elder with her book, the
younger with a bunch of flowers, are probably the prettiest
child-figures in England,[1] rivalled only, perhaps, by the
delicious little charity-school girls on the monument of
Olave Talbot (*ob.* 1685) at Salwarpe with their plain caps
and aprons and their innocent fresh faces ; the charity-
school boys in gowns and bands, shedding boisterous
tears on the monument of Frances, Duchess of Somerset,
in Westminster Abbey are grotesque by comparison.

Now and again the static character of these child-
figures is changed for a dynamic quality. On the
singular monument to the seventh Earl and Countess
of Thomond at Great Billing, where two exquisite
flying cherubs hold back a curtain to reveal a family
kneeling about an altar-tomb surmounted by the
inevitable swaddled babe, John Bushnell has grouped
seven other children, not as decorations but as persons.
The kneeling girls at the corner lean forward with
clasped hands as if at sight of a beatific vision, their
very draperies in movement ; the five little sisters
in front of the tomb are all in different postures, four
with linked arms, not to a pattern but as if catching at
each other, a fifth holding her prayer-book with both
hands and looking up from it. All are strangely unlike
the prim little figures on the Sackville tomb at Withyham by Bushnell's rival Cibber, who stand almost
as demurely as any mediæval weeper (Plate X).

When the child is the subject of the monument, the
varieties of conception, pose, and movement are infinite.
The brass effigy of Catherine, the five-year-old dumb
daughter of Henry III, made by Simon of Wells has
long since gone, along with the brasses of the young
daughters of Edward IV and Henry VII, once, like it,
in the Abbey ; for the latter Skelton wrote an epitaph.
Two child-tombs by Maximilian Colt, sculptor of the
great monument of Queen Elizabeth, yet remain :
Mary, daughter of James I, lies on her elbow on an

[1] Plate XVII.

altar-tomb, supported by four seated *amorini* ; Sophia,
her tiny sister, rests in a cradle near her, recalling that
touching figure of his little Lydia by John Dwight, the
Fulham potter-sculptor, some seventy years later.
Lydia's contemporary, little Rebekah Atkyns, at St.
Paul's, Clapham, with her bunch of flowers, her stiff
bodice, and round innocent face, is an exquisite figure ;
so is that toddling baby Mary Knightley at Tarporley,
holding the flowers which, local legend has it, she was
drowned in gathering, who, says her epitaph, " was
buried by her Aunt and Grandmother near ye place
of this Monument in wch her Memory also (as appears
by ye Figure at ye Feet) has a deserved share, for of such
is the Kingdom of God."

Now and again we have a grimmer symbolism. Young
Edward Shirburne of Mitton, the last heir of an ancient
name, walks with loose robe and flowing hair against
the background of a great mural monument, and
starts back from the skull and crossbones at his feet
(p. 27). But the only child of many hopes died often
at a tenderer age. Lady Margaret Legh at Fulham
holds on her knee the stiffly swaddled babe whose
birth cost her her life ; Mrs. Myddelton at Chirk clasps
her infant to her bosom ; but babes such as these are
not individualised. It is otherwise with two monuments commemorating the child of that great Lord
Mayor of London Sir Robert Clayton. One, an exquisite effigy on the vestry floor at Ickenham,[1] shows
us the babe lying, like Dwight's Lydia, but without a
cradle, a marvellous study by some unknown genius
of the peace of another world upon a baby-face. He
died " within a few Houres after his birth " on August
20, 1665 ; " Resurgam," adds the epitaph, " of such
are ye Kingdome of Heav'n." Forty years after, when
Sir Robert lost his wife and erected the vast monument
described elsewhere (p. 105), the babe was not forgotten, but carved by Richard Crutcher upon his
parents' tomb, lying between them in the infant pomp

[1] Plate XIX.

of lace-frilled frock and cap. Swaddling was not quite given up even later, as Hogarth's picture of Orator Henley Baptising shows us ; but here is evidence that some English babes at least were free to kick even in Queen Anne's day ; lesser emancipations have been thought worthy the historian's notice.

The long-clothes baby, unswaddled and in all the pomp of robes, is very rare. I have come across one instance only, and that, as might be expected, on one of the most remarkable costume pieces in England, the Savage monument at Elmley Castle, whose kneeling children have been already noticed. The tiny cap, the bib, the robe with panels of lace down the front, and dainty bows of ribbon at the waist might be of 1900 ; not so the tiny slashed sleeves gathered into a hem above the elbow, replicas in miniature of the lady's of the time. (Plate XVIII.) Whether the babe was removed from its swaddling-clothes for state occasions, or whether some happy children escaped their bondage in the 1630's, I cannot say ; the former possibly, since the swaddled babe is rarer in painting than in sculpture.

The childish monumental bust earlier than the seventeenth century I have not found, nor is it ever common. One or two of that age may, however, be noted, and many others must exist. There is little Edward Perry at Marholme, alluded to in Chapter IV, whose nose was broken in spite of his parents' appeal " to the Courteous Souldier " ; there are some pretty childish busts by Edward Marshall[1] at Tottenham ; there is Henry Cotton at Conington, great-grandson of Sir Robert, who died, an only child, at the age of fourteen. " He was the joy of his parents, and the delight of all who knew him," says his epitaph, " Innocent and Beautifull, as those Angells with whom He is now Singing the Praises of his Creator, God Blessed for ever." The bust of this fair boy, the only work we have signed " G. Gibbons Fec^t.," looks on us from his monument, flanked by garlands of flowers and doves

[1] P. 136,

perched upon crowns of immortality, and shows us
that there is another side to the age which we are apt
to look upon as the most brutal in our history. Two
young sisters lie at Conington also, dead in 1748, the
daughters of Dingley Askham, and their medallion
portraits, the work, I think, of Rysbrack, are upon the
tomb, which tells, in lines later added, that their sisters
lived till 1784–5.

At Cranborne is the effigy of a little boy, seated in
a niche in doublet, hose, and high boots, his chin supported on his hand.   "M.S. Desideratissimi capitis
Johannis Eliot," says the inscription, "qui dum hic
vernaculis literis incubuit, vi morbi oppressus concubuit
2 Februar. MDCXLI. At qualis adulescentulus,
quantae spei in aetate tam puerili vix uspiam majus
exemplum dotum denique naturae omnium, quas dum
arte sedulo et studiose perpolire conatur, supergressus
fere modum humanum angelorum inseritur choro."   A
Latin epigram follows, testifying to the powers of this
child of tender years, whose bunch of flowers is, one
may hope, not symbolic merely, but evidence of other
pursuits than those of Vernacular Literature.

A girl of fifteen, Elizabeth Smith, lies in St. Botolph's,
Aldgate, her charming head sculptured in profile by
Roubiliac ; but it is curious how little the medallion
form is used for children, to whom it is, as modern
French artists have discovered, peculiarly suited. There
is a baby by the same hand upon the Coningsby monument at Hope-under-Dinsmore, whose portrait, like
those of his parents, dead long years before, was probably
executed from a painting.   Children, not very childlike,
cluster round Rysbrack's Lord and Lady Foley at
Witley ; it is odd that the man who modelled the
exquisite portrait heads of the Beaufort family at
Badminton has failed to make these marble figures
equally convincing.

Banks's masterpiece, the Penelope Boothby at Ashbourne, is the most touching of memorials to a dear
and only child. She lies asleep, her hands touching

THE SAVAGE MONUMENT, ELMLEY CASTLE, SHOWING THE COSTUME OF THE EARLY YEARS
OF CHARLES I. AND A LONG CLOTHES BABY IN THE MOTHER'S ARMS.

PLATE XVIII.

THE CHILDREN OF THE SIXTH EARL OF
RUTLAND, BOTTESFORD. HOLDING
SKULLS, THE SYMBOLS OF DEATH.

PLATE XX.

facing p. 85.

THE ONLY SON OF SIR ROBERT
CLAYTON, ICKENHAM. PERHAPS
THE FINEST STUDY OF A BABE IN
ENGLISH ART.

PLATE XIX.

her face, in the muslin frock of daily life, the little
bare feet drawn up as if in uneasy sleep. Queen Charlotte burst into tears at sight of it in the Royal Academy,
and it deserves its fame ; but it had a rival once in a work
destroyed in the Irish troubles of 1921–2. In 1791 the
Hon. Hercules Langford Rowley erected a monument
to his granddaughter the Hon. Mary Pakenham, whom
Banks represented kneeling in prayer, her dog by her
side, on a pedestal adorned with reliefs of Scripture
subjects. The work was placed in a mausoleum at
Summerhill House, co. Cork,[1] but the mausoleum
becoming ruinous, the work was transferred to the
house, which was unhappily burnt down. One of
the panels, we read, represented " two angels opening
bolted doors and releasing a man from prison. Beneath
is the legend,

> I was in prison, and ye visited me."

That the panel in the Soane Museum usually described
as the Release of St. Peter is in fact the model for this
lost work there can, I think, be little doubt.

Chantrey's most famous group, the Sleeping Children
at Lichfield, has had more than its share of admiration.
It is pretty, but neither modelling nor carving is first-
rate, and though it was long thought the extreme of
pathos, that pathos has a Dickens-like quality to-day.
The tragedy of the grown son or daughter can only be
touched on here, though examples are many and noble ;
the grandest of all, Roubiliac's Dormer monument at
Quainton, with the father and mother lamenting over
the dead body of their only son, may have suggested
the latest of such elaborate groups, Chantrey's Mariamne
Johnes at Hafod, on which father and mother—the
former a noble study in realistic portraiture—bend with
set faces over their dying child. The work was unfinished when Thomas Johnes was ruined, and stayed
in Chantrey's studio until the Duke of Newcastle, the

---

[1] There is a sketch in vol. viii of the Irish Memorials Association,
p. 614 ; for this reference I am indebted to Mr. W. G. Strickland.

next owner of Hafod, paid for it and set it, to his eternal honour, in the place designed for it.

Flaxman has given us the ideal schoolboy on Dr. Warton's monument at Winchester, the family group in more than one combination—notably in the Fitzharris monument at Christchurch, a sort of Hoppner group in marble which unfortunately exhibits something of that curious lack of power over his material when working in the round on a large scale on which Cunningham comments. Nollekens in a notable monument to Mrs. Howard of Corby has a touching group of Religion bending over a mother and child, but here again the surface and handling are curiously unsatisfactory when compared with earlier work. The sculptor's " ghost " [1] has come between ; the master's hand has never touched the marble ; the result is a deadness lacking in earlier and far less famous works, such as the splendid Covert tomb at Slaugham, with its dignified Renaissance detail and its thirteen kneeling sons and daughters, the only one to die in infancy being sandwiched between his father and his elder brother, where he supports himself, child-fashion, by clinging to the ample folds of his father's trunk-hose. The otherwise unknown sculptor, Flynton, shows herein a sympathy with little children hardly to be found elsewhere in 1579. This noble work cost only £30.

These *imagines innocentium*, then, are worth more than a mere casual study. Those here chosen are but examples, perhaps not even the best examples, since books are almost useless for the purpose, and personal knowledge must of necessity be limited. But they may serve to show how rich a field of interest awaits the investigator, what singular sidelights upon the life of the time emerge from the study of the children of our monuments, from the infant dying as soon as born to the youth cut off at the threshold of a noble manhood and, like Sir Robert Dormer's son, laid out for burial before his father's eyes.

[1] In this case Nollekens's assistant Goblet, according to J. T. Smith.

CHAPTER VIII

THE SCENIC BAS-RELIEF

The bas-relief upon a monument, the " rich relievo " of Dart's poem (p. 53), is usually narrative, explanatory of some incident in the life or death of the subject of the monument, the record of some memorable crisis in his history, and is usually, though not always, appended as it were to the bust or effigy of the dead man.

Thus, though the effigy of Aymer de Valence reclines upon his tomb, above, on the canopy, is his figure as he appeared in life, armed and on horseback ; but such reliefs are distinctly rare in our mediæval tombs. By Jacobean times they had become fairly frequent : we need only go to Barking to see Sir Charles Montagu, brother of Henry, first Earl of Manchester, dying on the field of battle, his page holding his horse at the door of his tent ; to the Abbey, to see Stone's Sir George Holles fighting in the Netherland Wars ; between them in date comes Stone's tomb of the founder of the Charterhouse, with a relief showing him or another in the act of preaching to the Poor Brothers. John Schoerman's monument to Justice Shallow's grandson, already alluded to as an instance of the scholar's monument, has not only a noble effigy, but a panel showing him riding in charming rural scenery which can hardly be other than Charlcote Chase itself, of which it is probably the only seventeenth-century representation. That Shakespearean commentators have left it unnoticed would be astonishing, were anything but a monument in question.

Scenes from the life of an ancestor are sometimes, though rarely, represented on a monument : thus, the death of John Hampden on Chalgrove Field appears on the monument of his great-grandson of the same name at Great Hampden. But such cases are rare, and the great majority of these reliefs are contemporary representations of the scene depicted, and most of them belong to the eighteenth century. Towards the end of that century, however, such gospel scenes as the Good Samaritan begin to take their place,[1] and the historic bas-relief expires with the Oxford Movement, to which such representations of human glory were wholly alien.

Sometimes the scene is general, sometimes individualised ; and if some of the earlier examples are set high up on the tomb, it becomes customary at a later date to place them on the base, where, in the case of statues, they were of course bound to be. Thus the doctor visiting his patients figures on the pedestal of Roubiliac's Sir Thomas Molyneux at Armagh, the scene of Hough's expulsion from Magdalen by James II on the Bishop's monument at Worcester ; a sea scene, to indicate that he was Governor of the Leeward Islands, adorned Bacon's lost monument to Lord Lavington in Antigua ; an actual engagement in which Wager captured the Spanish treasure-ships in the West Indies may be seen on that Admiral's monument in Westminster Abbey.

Very few people pay much attention to these reliefs, fewer still realise their interest as contemporary records of the events depicted. Yet their scale is large enough to give us a picture of the rigging of a Georgian ship, the dress of a British soldier or sailor, or the details of a Stuart coach more vivid than that supplied by medals or engravings, more true to life than such fancy pictures of battles as hang in the Painted Hall at Greenwich. There are worse ways of spending an hour than in examining a few of those in Westminster Abbey not as yet mentioned here.

[1] The earliest I know is that to Jacob Bosanquet (ob. 1767), in Bath Abbey, an exquisite work probably by Rysbrack, certainly not by Roubiliac (ob. 1762), to whom it has been attributed.

We may begin with Captain Philip de Sausmarez, killed fighting bravely under Admiral Hawke off Finisterre in 1747 : his monument by Cheere, a delightful baroque work, a drawing for which is in the Victoria and Albert Museum, bears a spirited relief of the battle, with the French and English ships engaged at close quarters.[1] By way of contrast we may take the death of the hero of Ticonderoga, Colonel Roger Townshend, killed at the age of twenty-eight, with the Fort itself in the background ; and for the sake of the hero and of Stevenson's poem, we shall forgive the solecism of French and English soldiers in Roman dress.   Yet it is really a fine thing in itself, as even Flaxman, to whom most works of the period were anathema, admitted ; and it was " cut " by Eckstein, one of the " clever fellows " whom, said Nollekens, Carter kept to do his work, the two names for once appearing side by side, though a mere assistant was rarely honoured by having his signature appended to what was frequently his work and not his master's.

Would you see what Trichinopoli was like, when Stringer Lawrence held it for eighteen months against the French, and thereby paved the way for Clive's yet greater victory at Plassey three years later ?   Look at his monument by W. Tyler, R.A.   Or the taking of Quebec ?   There, on Capizzoldi's relief affixed to Wilton's colossal Wolfe, you may follow the whole heroic story, from the Crossing of the St. Lawrence to the Heights of Abraham.   Some vandal destroyed the very interesting reliefs on Bushnell's monument to Sir Palmes Fairborne : they were there in 1754 ; they were gone in 1816 ; and that is all we know about it. But they represented the siege of Tangier in 1680, and the heroic death of its young Governor, and not Dryden's epitaph itself can atone for the wanton removal of scenes so interesting.

The one exception to the rule that such reliefs are generally gnored by the visitor is the monument

[1] Plate XXI.

depicting the death of Major André, designed by Robert Adam, executed by Van Gelder, and erected by George III, which Americans at least make a point of seeing, and which we all know from Lamb's protest to Southey against its mutilation having been made the pretext for shutting up the Abbey. But alas! though the uniforms, both English and American, are accurate enough, the heads of George Washington and Major André have been stolen again and again. Have the restorers followed Adam's drawings in the Soane Museum? Not, I think, as closely as they might have, which is a pity, seeing that the said drawings have almost as much beauty and at least as much historical value as the lost heads themselves. (Plate XXIV.)

An earlier scene from the American War of Independence is to be seen at Great Bookham, on the monument of the young hero Cornet Geary, who fell in a skirmish in 1776 at the age of four-and-twenty. "Entrusted with a command which he executed with singular spirit," says the epitaph, "he was attacked on his return by a large body of the rebels, who lay in wait for him in a wood, and killed whilst gallantly fighting at the head of his little troop." Here are no Greeks and Romans, but English and American soldiers in the dress of their day, and it is a thousand pities that a scene so interesting has remained unknown to historians. Neither the relief nor the bust of Geary above appear to be signed, and conjecture as to the artist is useless at this date.

Returning to the Abbey, we may take a naval relief or two for a change. To Admiral Wager's exploit we have already alluded; it is as spirited a work of Scheemaker's as we possess. Taylor's vast monument to Captain Cornewall contains, when you can hit on it in that vast conglomeration of scenery and history combined, a really excellent scene of his fight off Toulon in 1743, just as Captain Edward Cooke's fight with the *La Forte* frigate in Balasore Roads in 1799 is dramatised by the younger Bacon nearly half a century later.

Among miscellaneous reliefs in the Abbey that which most arouses curiosity is Quellin's on the base of his fine monument to that unworthy profligate Tom Thynne of Longleat (*ob.* 1685), depicting his murder in his coach when driving down the Haymarket by three hirelings of Count Königsmarck, who hoped, once Thynne was out of the way, to marry his child-widow, the heiress of the Percys. Fate reserved her for the proud Duke of Somerset, the ghost of whose monument—for it never existed in fact—I have pursued round Salisbury Cathedral [1]; and it was her conduct in never daring to sit down in his presence which was held up as a model to the Duchess her successor, a mere Churchill, though her father was the Duke of Marlborough. On the Thynne monument the details of coach, costume, etc., are very curious, though the taste which permitted the intrusion of a brutal murder scene in the Abbey itself is more than questionable.[2] It is pleasant to turn to Cheere's attractive monument to Dean Willcocks, Innocent VIII's "beloved heretic," in whose time the Western towers of the Abbey were built and who loved them so dearly that he begged they should be depicted on his tomb. It was real feeling, too—the honour paid by the public to a righteous man—which prompted the erection of Moore's monument to Jonas Hanway. It is not a great work of art in any sense, but the figure of Britannia presenting sailors' uniforms to the outcast boys of our London streets recalls one of the most enduring of his many good deeds, his foundation of the Marine Society for helping friendless lads to sea. One wishes, though, that there had been some allusion to his work for saving parish children from the horrors of the baby-farm. Sixty-four out of seventy-eight infants perished in a single year in one London workhouse; thirty-seven died out of forty-eight in another; five children only survived of twenty-three entrusted to a " nurse's " care; in some cases

---

[1] A description of it, sculptor and all, is given in the *Dictionary of National Biography*; but it does not exist, never has existed, and ought to be deleted. [2] Plate XXIV.

even every child was dead by the end of a year. At
his own expense Hanway got two Acts through Parliament to remedy these ghastly evils, one of them directing
the publication of statistics, the other arranging for
the nursing of children under six " under special guar-
dians, at a sufficient distance " from the heart of London.
The foundation of the Magdalene Hospital and of
several Lock hospitals, improvements in the lot of
chimney-sweepers, were among his righteous deeds ;
and if one cannot expect to find the homely wisdom of
the populariser of the umbrella commemorated on his
tomb, the rest should not have been omitted from the
inscription at least.

The monument to Dr. Hales, the physiologist and
chemist, is an odd work. He is buried at Teddington
under the plainest of tablets, and his monument in the
Abbey bears a relief representing Religion and Botany
supporting a medallion portrait with a globe below
upon which the Four Winds are blowing. Hales was
the inventor of the ventilator, and his invention deserves record ; but on the singular memorial by Wilton,
the sculptor of Wolfe's cenotaph, the allegory is so
obscure that without this explanation the relief is un-
intelligible. It was Augusta, Princess of Wales and
mother of George III, who erected the memorial to
her neighbour and protégé ; but adequately to represent his invention would seem to pass the wit of
man.

Almost all the monuments in St. Paul's belong
to the worst period of English sculpture, and the
reliefs on them are mostly negligible, though often
historically interesting. But up and down the country
will be found a hundred curious and pretty things.

Peter Pett, the master shipbuilder—one of the family
whom we meet in Pepys—has the bows of a battle-
ship on his monument at Deptford [1] ;   the Countess
of Derby sits dispensing alms to beggars under a tree at

---

[1] It may well be his masterpiece, the *Sovereign of the Seas*, for which
John and Matthias Christmas did the carving (p. 136).

Boxgrove[1]; the Duke of Marlborough receives the surrender of Marshal Tallard on his monument at Blenheim, and the relief is a marvel of delicacy and historical correctness.[2]

All these things are subsidiary, a part only of a larger whole ; but they are surely fascinating. It is odd that Grinling Gibbons did so little in this kind. His genius for relief has given us the finest decorative woodwork we possess, and his historical scenes, such as the Crucifixion, which Evelyn found him copying from Tintoretto, the Stoning of St. Stephen, once at Canons and now in the Victoria and Albert Museum, and the Calling of St. Matthew, now in Wiltshire, are every whit as great. But on his monuments the historical panel in low relief does not exist, so far as I can ascertain ; the nearest approach to it is in the carvings of the eighteen children of Viscount Campden, at Exton, and here, after all, he was only following a familiar mediæval precedent expressed in the idiom of his day. A nameless contemporary is responsible for the quaint and curious reliefs, in the manner of Bushnell, upon the monument to Sir Edward Winter (*ob.* 1686) at the old parish church of Battersea :

> Alone, unarmed, a tyger he opprest,
> And crush'd to death the monster of a beast,
> Full fifty Mounted Moors he overthrew,
> Dispers'd the rest. What more coud Sampson do ?

There he is, wig and all, engaged in the unequal combat of the epitaph, and the Tyger is obviously having the worst of it. The bust of this Porthos of a man, a fine thing in itself, is all the more interesting for the enlivening exploits depicted below.

Sometimes, though rarely, relief is successfully combined with figures in the round. The noblest example

---

[1] I should like to recant the theory expressed in the *Architect* in 1922 that this is a work of Rysbrack ; the likeness to the Townshend monument is such that we may safely ascribe it to Carter and Eckstein. I have to thank my son for the correction.

[2] Plate XXIII. The marble is at Blenheim, the lovely model, one of Rysbrack's best works, at the Soane Museum.

in London, and one of the greater things of English art,
is on Bacon's monument of Thomas Guy in the chapel
of his hospital, to whose façade (it was before the altera-
tions in which Bacon himself had a share) Guy himself
points the sick man at his side. The delicate relief
of this background, with bearers carrying a stretcher
towards its Doors of Healing, may sound grotesque
enough ; in fact it is worthy of the figure of Guy himself,
or of the sick man, whose head, under the title of *Sickness*,
was executed in replica as Bacon's Diploma work on
his election to the full honours of the Royal Academy,
and is one of the few fine things in that melancholy
collection of English sculpture. (Plate XXXI.)

The trouble, when we write of these reliefs, lies in
knowing where to leave off, so great is their interest,
so little known their fascination. But these may serve
to show how much new pleasure is within our reach,
if we will only take the trouble to accept it. The moral
of Eyes and No Eyes is eternal, and if we are wise, we
shall not let any guide-book prate of Good period and
Bad, any Ruskin-like denunciation of the art of whole
centuries deter us from using ours. Only by so doing
shall we learn how much there is to see.

It is a very odd fact that Reynolds disapproved of
the bas-relief, even though he admitted that the ancients
themselves were outdone by " certain single groups in
basso-relievo " by modern sculptors How, after this
admission, he reconciled it to his common sense to main-
tain that " the representing the effects of perspective in
bas-relief " was an " imaginary improvement of the
moderns " it is hard to say ; but it is probable that
the lessening use of relief on English monuments and
even on English mantelpieces, another fruitful field
of the sculptor's art, after 1790 may be attributed to
the influence of his opinion.[1]

---

[1] The Tenth Discourse was delivered in December 1780, and we must
allow time for his opinions to penetrate the public. See Chapter V.

CHAPTER IX

THE SCULPTOR AND THE ARCHITECT

It was long before the functions of sculptor and architect were really differentiated. Colt, Christmas, Stone, Bernard Johnson, Pierce, and Cibber are among those who in the seventeenth century combined the functions of both ; this chapter will show how even in the eighteenth the architect in the course of his practice was called upon as a matter of course to design monuments to be carried out by sculptors of distinction.[1]

This is no new observation. " In England," says Allan Cunningham, in his *Life of Roubiliac* (1830), " our architects long preserved their ascendancy, and as late as the middle of the last century dictated to sculptors with a boldness of which we have no notion nowadays, and which was probably only tolerated there because our figure-makers were poor friendless foreigners." The statement, as we have seen, needs modification ; but it is interesting to set beside it a passage from the Vertue MSS. The antiquary is speaking of Rysbrack's early work, especially his admirable portrait busts of Lord Nottingham, Sir Thomas Hewitt, and of " Mr. Gibbs, Architect, he who from the time of his first coming to England [October 1720] has much imploy'd him, but has always done it for his own advantage, not for encouragement, that the poor man [Rysbrack, that is] has opened his mind to me and told me of his extravagant exactions on his labour, that he could not possibly live had not other business come in to help him, of

---

[1] Herein lies the difference between these monuments and those designed by men like Sir John Soane but executed by nameless underlings.

more profit. An instance of this is now in the Monument of Mr. Prior [in Poets' Corner] which he is now about. The Statues at length as big as the life representing Poesi [and History], he will give him no more than 35 pounds for each Statue to be cut in Marble when others have above a hundred pounds, and Mr. Gibbs is to have of My Lord Harley upwards of hundred pounds for each of the Statues. Many other things of this kind he has done by him.

" Tis an unreasonable gripeing Usage for a most Ingenious artist in his Way, for far more of merit than Gibbs ever will be master of." [1]

But there were worse cases at a later date. Gibbs's shabbiness was far excelled by Nollekens, who received 3,000 guineas for his Pitt, and after patching it together out of small pieces of marble, gave the actual carver only a poor £300. Yet Gibbs's conduct evidently scandalised Vertue, and as he was so much in touch with the artists of his day, we may take it that " the poor friendless foreigner " was usually better treated in the 1720's.

Among the monuments executed by Rysbrack for Gibbs we may name the Ben Jonson, Smith, and Freind in the Abbey, the Robert Stuart in St. Margaret's, Westminster, and the Bridgman at Aston, near Birmingham ; the drawings for the last two are in the Victoria and Albert Museum. Francis Bird executed the Newcastle monument in the Abbey after Gibbs's designs, Scheemaker that of Mrs. Bovey : we should remember this forgotten branch of Gibbs's activities when we look at St. Martin's and the Radcliffe Library.

The Admiralty screen, the figures of which were carved by Spang, and the late Devonshire House are familiar instances of Kent's work as architect, and since the days of Hogarth and Walpole his productions in other fields, ranging from altar-pieces to dead trees planted in Kensington Gardens to give a realistic effect, have been mercilessly ridiculed ; yet his monu-

[1] Quoted in the *Architect*, May 3, 1922, from B.M. Add. MSS.

MONUMENT OF CAPTAIN DE SAUS-
MAREZ, WESTMINSTER ABBEY. BY SIR
HENRY CHEERE. FINE BAROQUE WORK,
WITH RELIEF SHOWING THE BATTLE
IN WHICH DE SAUSMAREZ PERISHED.

PLATE XXI.

MONUMENT OF SIR JOHN AND LADY COTTON,
LANDWADE. SCHOOL OF WILLIAM AND CORNELIUS
CURE.

PLATE XXII.

facing p. 96.

TERRA COTTA MODEL FOR THE BAS-RELIEF ON THE DUKE OF MARLBOROUGH'S MONUMENT AT BLENHEIM, SOANE MUSEUM. BY J. M. RYSBRACK, SHOWING THE SURRENDER OF MARSHALL TALLARD TO THE DUKE OF MARLBOROUGH AT BLENHEIM.

PLATE XXIII.

facing p. 97.

mental designs, the Abbey Shakespeare excepted, have been virtually ignored. The Shakespeare and its variant at Wilton were executed by Scheemaker after his design ; Rysbrack did the monuments of Newton [1] and Stanhope, the former of which Vertue calls in 1731 " a noble and Elegant work of Mr. Michael Rysbrack, and much to his Reputation tho the design and drawing of it on paper was poor enough ; yet for that only Mr. Kent is honoured with his name on it [*Pictor et Archit. inven*[t]] which if it had been delivered to any other Sculptor beside Rysbrack, he might have been glad to have his name omitted." [2]   Outside the Abbey I have noted Kent's interesting tablet erected by Berkeley to Mrs. Anne Wainwright (1717) in Chester Cathedral, with its Quattrocento-like scheme of two cherubs holding a great swag ; the monument to Elizabeth Stanley in Holy Rood Church, Southampton, with an epitaph by James Thomson ; and the extraordinary urn some 14 feet high at Ashby-de-la-Zouche, bearing an exquisite medallion portrait of the famous Countess of Huntingdon in Vandyck dress, veiled and resting her head on her clasped hands. Both the last-named were the work of Rysbrack, and as an authentic representation of Selina has long been a *desideratum*, the importance of this singular medallion will readily be seen.

Another architect who—though the fact seems to have escaped notice—designed monuments was Giacomo Leoni, a protégé of Lord Burlington, who was responsible for Bramham Park, Moor Park, and other great country houses, and who also designed the tombs of Sir Richard Pigott at Quainton, Bucks, and Daniel Pulteney in the Abbey Cloisters, both works of considerable dignity, the latter known to be, the former almost certainly, carved by Rysbrack.[3]

[1] Plate XII.
[2] This stricture cannot apply to the only known drawing, by Rysbrack, in the British Museum, which is singularly beautiful; Kent's original design must have been much inferior.
[3] The Pulteney is mentioned as Rysbrack's by his friend Charles Rogers.

7

We know nothing of the J. Potter who signs " Arch^t "
on the admirable monument of James Cart (*ob.* 1706)
in St. Mary-le-Bow, executed by S. Tufnell, a sculptor
as unknown as he was competent ; and curiously little
of another man, at once a sculptor and an architect,
William Tyler, a foundation member of the Royal
Academy, who was responsible for many excellent
monuments. His busts of Provost Smith in the ante-
chapel of Queen's College, Oxford, his Charles Holland
at Chiswick, and his Admiral Storr, Zachary Pearce,
and General Stringer Lawrence in the Abbey are sound
and excellent works, though his bust of Martin Folkes
there is better than the attendant allegories ; his Barton
Booth, also in the Abbey, has a delightful medallion
portrait, nor are such fine mural monuments as those at
Hitchin, Southwark Cathedral, Marchwiel, Bletchingley,
St. George's, Stamford, and Belton unworthy of the
best traditions of his immediate predecessors.

With Sir William Chambers and Robert Adam, James
Stuart and George Dance, Junior, we come to names
more famous ; yet the monuments they designed seem
to have passed almost unnoticed. Chambers was responsible for two important works, both executed by
Joseph Wilton, R.A., but we shall probably be safe
in assuming that the R.A.'s worked as colleagues and
not as master and man on the monuments in question,
those of the Earl and Countess of Mountrath in the
Abbey (much cut down by restorers) and that of the
third Duke of Bedford at Chenies.

James, or " Athenian," Stuart, to give him the name
by which he is best known, was not only a pioneer of
classical archæology in England, but a very competent
architect. Eight monuments at least exist from his
design, all works of interest, four executed by the elder
Scheemaker and four by that sculptor's son Thomas.
Two of the first, those of Admiral Watson and Viscount
Howe, are in the Abbey, and, like the two grand monuments at Wimpole to members of the Yorke family, are
in the mixed tradition of the Renaissance, as are his

son's monuments to the Somers Cocks family at Eastnor [1] and that to the fourth Earl of Shaftesbury at Wimborne St. Giles. There is delicate classic detail, however, in the younger Scheemakers' monument to Wedgwood's partner Bentley at Chiswick, which has far more of Stuart's classical training behind it. [2]

Robert Adam was more catholic in his choice of sculptors. He employed Rysbrack on the Curzon and Boscawen monuments at Kedleston and St. Michael Penkivel; Carter and Eckstein on the Townshend monument in the Abbey; Michael Spang on that of James Thomson; Roubiliac's pupil Read on that of the Duchess of Northumberland, both also there; and that obscure but prolific sculptor, Peter Matthias Van Gelder, on the world-famous relief of Major André (Plate XXIV) and on the grandiose monument to Mary, Duchess of Montagu (*ob.* 1775) at Warkton. [3] Some of these works, notably the Curzon tomb, are purely Renaissance in manner, and only the drawings prove the designs to be Adam's work. The Northumberland tomb is full of fine classic detail; but the great Montagu monument, a segment of a vast circular temple adorned with delicate reliefs, cries out *Aut Adam aut nemo*, though the figures of the angel and the mourners over the Duchess's urn are less distinctive.

Of the younger George Dance as designer of monuments only one example can be cited, the tablet to Scipio and Alexander Duroure in the Abbey cloisters. An obscure architect of the period, John Plaw, to whom we owe Old Paddington church, designed a monument to Peter Dore (*ob.* 1781) in Christ Church, Newgate Street, which was carried out by Robert Chambers,

[1] Removed to the church tower by Sir Gilbert Scott in 1848.

[2] Drawing at the Victoria and Albert Museum. The monument by the same sculptor to the Freeman family at Braughing, Herts, is, my son tells me, practically a duplicate. Thomas Scheemakers, unlike his father, always retained the final " s " in his name.

[3] Plate XXVI. Cited as Roubiliac's by Le Roy de Ste Croix in his life of that sculptor. Illustrated in Hyett's book on Northamptonshire monuments and by the writer in the *Architect* for 1922, where, however, Adam's share in the work is not recognised.

the designer of many mural monuments and tablets between 1760 and 1790, a " stainer " of marble and an enthusiast for Hebrew. It is almost safe to say indeed that any monument of the period bearing Hebrew letters is Chambers's work, whether it is signed or not, and his talent was a delicate and remarkable one [1] ; the example after Plaw seems to be the only one in which he carried out the designs of another man, and there may have been some personal reason for the choice.

It is clear then that there is some truth in Cunningham's statement as to the importance of architects in eighteenth-century sculpture ; for the sixteenth and seventeenth centuries our evidence is less certain, since the functions of sculpture and architecture were less distinct than they afterwards became. Sculptors of the generation of the Johnsons worked for architects on the great mantelpieces and the external sculpture of such houses as Hengrave and Aston Hall [2] ; Colt, who did Lord Salisbury's monument at Hatfield, was assuredly responsible for much of the woodwork at Hatfield House. In the next century a man like Stone combined the functions both of a sculptor and architect, as did also Pierce and Cibber ; but this is a different matter. It is a question whether on one occasion, however, Wren himself did not design a monument. A drawing in a volume of Wren drawings at the Soane Museum, described as the monument of " John Dillenius in St. Peter's in ye East," suggests that Wren, who probably knew Dillen at Oxford, had a hand in his tablet, and the point is curious at least. If we can add our proudest name to the list of famous architects who undertook the work of designing monuments, it is a

[1] The tablet to the Earl of Stafford (ob. 1762) in Westminster Abbey " invented and stained by Robert Chambers " is a good example ; for once it has no Hebrew lettering, but typical instances with that lettering are at Horsted Keynes and Dover, and the mural monument to Zachary Pearce at Bromley, Kent. An interesting letter as to the Stafford monument is given in Nichols's *Literary Anecdotes*, viii, p. 710.

[2] The mantelpieces at Aston Hall are most probably from the Johnsons' studio, and Gerard Christmas did the external sculptures of old Northumberland House.

MONUMENT OF THOMAS THYNNE OF LONGLEAT, WEST-
MINSTER ABBEY. BY ARNOLD QUELLIN, AN ASSISTANT
OF GRINLING GIBBONS. THE BAS-RELIEF SHOWS HIM
IN HIS COACH, ASSASSINATED BY THREE RUFFIANS IN
PALL MALL, HIRED BY COUNT KONIGSMARCK.

PLATE XXV.

facing p. 100.

MONUMENT OF MAJOR ANDRÉ, WESTMIN-
STER ABBEY. DESIGNED BY ROBERT ADAM.
EXECUTED BY P. M. VAN GELDER. HEADS
OF ANDRÉ AND WASHINGTON MODERN.

PLATE XXIV.

MONUMENT TO MARY, THIRD DUCHESS OF MONTAGU.
WARKTON. DESIGNED BY ROBERT ADAM, EXECUTED BY
P. M. VAN GELDER.

PLATE XXVI.

facing p. 101.

further and most convincing argument for the importance of monumental art in England at the time.[1]

A few architects who sign their works in this field " fecit," and therefore presumably did not call on sculptors to carry out their designs, may also be named.

William Halfpenny, perhaps the most prolific writer of architectural books of the eighteenth century, is best known as the earliest introducer of Chinese motives into English building. He was an admirable example of the working builder of the age, who knew all about the Orders but was content to give plans and estimates for modest houses and even cottages, as well as mansions with a hundred-foot frontage and a courtyard or two costing £3,000 [2] ; but he too dabbled in monumental sculpture. His Mrs. Anne Dash at Isleworth is so large, dignified, and well carved that it might well have been assigned to Rysbrack ; yet, in the words of Cowper's friend Mat Lloyd in 1758, it was, like the *Chinoiseries* he laughed at, " From Halfpenny's exact designs."

Sir John Soane designed his own mausoleum as well as other tombs, and many architectural works of the age contain designs for such things, whose authors future research may identify, though the sculptors' names are probably gone for ever. It can have been no nameless men to whom we owe, for instance, the series of altar-tombs to successive Bishops of London in the churchyard at Fulham,[3] and now and again a country churchyard will abound in works of exquisite proportion, from one hand or studio clearly, whose authorship is now forgotten. There is a series of sarcophagus tombs of the finest proportions and most delightful Greek detail at Old Shoreham, Sussex, which suggest the hand of an architect perfectly acquainted

---

[1] The same volume, however, contains a drawing for a monument carried out long afterwards at Arkesden, Essex, with which Wren can have had nothing to do.

[2] An excellent nine-roomed house of two storeys cost £114 18s. 11d. in stone, or £141 10s. in brick, in the blessed year 1751.

[3] That of Bishop Sherlock is signed " John Vardy *Delin*," so that Vardy was among the architects responsible for designing monuments.

with the Erechtheum ; they are carried out in a local stone, and it is not perhaps an accident that headstones and tablets of the twentieth century surmounted by palmettes and acroteria are to be found in many church-yards within five-and-twenty miles, some of the most noteworthy, at Bletchingley, over the Surrey border, actually bearing twentieth-century dates. As there is no notable classical building near, it seems as if the tradition of some architect or architectural pattern-book of the Greek Revival were still potent in the local masons' yards, especially as large-scale monuments of 1790–1830 are singularly lacking in the neighbourhood.

The signature of the younger Wyatt may be found on many monuments ; that of Richard Blore occa-sionally occurs ; and Gilbert Scott and his pupil Street were responsible for several ecclesiastical tombs in the mediæval manner. But the old partnership between designer and sculptor was dissolved, and we come back to the complaint made by Vertue two centuries ago, that the architect gets the glory for "noble and elegant" works which owe their chief merit to the sculptor.

CHAPTER X

THE NEED OF UNDERSTANDING

IT may be helpful here to discuss in some detail a few representative monuments not, as hitherto, as illustrations of particular aspects, but as wholes, that we may better understand the sculptor's meaning and the way in which his work expresses the spirit of the age. The lack of such knowledge has led to the most extraordinary legends and misunderstandings, largely because the artistic idiom is now unfamiliar. A few instances of this may serve as warnings against accepting local legends at their face value ; but the possible importance of such legends is finally and conclusively vindicated by the history of the statue of Clement Spelman, already more than once alluded to.

We may begin with two monuments of the reign of Charles I, embodying one the very spirit of Little Gidding, the other that of the *Hydriotaphia*.

In the little church of Isfield, Sussex, is an enchanting chapel rich in linenfold panelling and stately pews enshrining four great monuments, one an Elizabethan altar-tomb, two others recording the memory of the Shirleys who served Henry VIII, the fourth that of Sir John Shirley (*ob.* 1631) and his two wives, a masterpiece of the great English school of alabaster workers. On the base kneel exquisite little figures of their children, their names inscribed above : Anne, Thomas, John—a tiny figure close beside his brother with whom, says the epitaph, he was " called into heaven "—Jane, Cicelie, Elizabeth, Charitie, Hannah, and Mary, each lovelier than the last. The epitaph records the memory

103

of a perfect woman in language worthy of the Authorised
Version :

> Her pitty was the clothing of the poore,
> Her piety the mother of her practice,
> Her devotions were her daily offerings to God,
> Her mercy sure against condemnation.
> And all her minutes were but steppes to heaven.

For a contrast let us return to that strange monument
of Sir John Denham at Egham, in its incongruous setting,
than which it would be hard to find a more perfect
expression of the ideals of the Greek Revival as applied
to ecclesiastical architecture. The ceiling, the walls,
the very pews are stencilled in Greek or Pompeian
patterns ; even the doors are simplified from those of
the Erechtheum, and the monuments by Flaxman and
Baily within the chancel rails are purely, and in their
way quite exquisitely, classical. Only the floral cushion
at the altar-rails, woolwork of the Regency as fresh in
colour and design as it was a century ago, shows the
least trace of any other taste. Over the galleries are
a few simple tablets, mostly of classical form. To
reach the Denham monuments we ascend by the fine
sweep of the gallery stairs, where, on the blank wall
opposite, we shall find Sir John's wives, two matronly
figures, one holding a child, a Rembrandt in the round,
and near it that haunting figure of Sir John himself.[1]
Præterita sperno, runs the legend, and the risen form,
shaking itself free of its cerements, answers the trumpet-
call and aspires to the *Vita perfecta* of the now illegible
tablet behind. From the charnel-house below rise
other figures, the newly dead and those whose bones
alone are left. Inside the folding doors beyond the
galleries is the smug church consecrated in 1820, " all
one magnificent apartment " ; outside, as in a Court
of the Gentiles, is this counterpart of Addison's vision
of the Day " when we shall all be contemporaries, and
make our appearance together."

It was largely the assertion of human dignities and

[1] Plate XXVII.

honours in the House of God which offended the protagonists of the Oxford Movement and which has
coloured all later accounts of eighteenth-century
monuments. If we analyse two of the largest in
some detail, we shall be better able to judge the
artist's meaning.

Of the infant on the Clayton tomb at Bletchingley
we have already spoken (p. 82) ; on the tomb itself
the guide-books have lavished more abuse than would
seem to have fallen to the lot of any other single work.
Against a vast architectural background with a broken
pediment Sir Robert stands in the robes of Lord Mayor
of London, holding a scroll and looking towards the
wife in whose honour he erected the monument. *Quando
invenies parem*, runs the inscription underneath her
statue, that of the Complete Dowager, with brooch
and bracelet and stately Queen Anne dress, well-cut
features, puffy wrinkled skin, and an indefinable air
of good breeding. Between them lies their only child,
the infant with cap and lace-frilled baby frock whom
we have also seen at Ickenham (p. 82). Ugly, pompous,
vainglorious, are the epithets heaped upon the work ;
yet the husband is turning towards the love of his
youth, his eyes seem to watch her very movements.
The work is the romance of a lifelong devotion, erected
by the husband himself ; and if the cherubs to right
and left weep marble tears, the convention may be
forgiven for the unflattered faithful faces of man and
wife. Even the mayoral insignia on the central panel
of the base were put there, one is sure, because Lady
Clayton was proud that her husband was Lord Mayor,
and the work is superlatively fine, as Aubrey said,
whether we look at the architectural setting or the
forms and faces of mother and child ; yet the
Richard Crutcher who signs it is utterly unknown, and
his work derided in every recent history of Surrey.

Sic transit gloria mundi ran the legend once to be
read upon the robes which lie upon the edge of Denham's
sculptured tomb ; it should be writ large upon such a

mausoleum as that of the Duke of Chandos in St.
Lawrence, Whitchurch. Timon's Villa has gone ; its
chapel has become a parish church ; and Timon stands
upon his tomb in his neglected mausoleum, an embodi-
ment of the vanity of human greatness.

The church itself is as he left it, rich in colour and
most admirably cared for, with frescoes by Bellucci
to right and left of the altar, an altar-piece with a
Nativity and Pietà, and a copy of Raphael's Trans-
figuration glowing on the ceiling above the ducal
pew at the west end. Handel's organ, dating from the
days when he was the Duke's Choirmaster, is there ;
all that the Duke did for glory not his own is still
unaltered. But enter the burying-place of that almost
Prince and see the change. Torn banners hang below
the damp-stained roof ; blurred and blistered frescoes
on walls and ceiling show tokens of decay ; the marble
floor is discoloured with penetrating wet. At the end,
facing the iron screen through whose doors you enter,
rises one of the most splendid monuments which even
the eighteenth century commissioned. Against a temple-
like structure surmounted by urns and a canopy
crowned by a coronet stands the Duke in periwig and
Roman armour, his sword by his side, his right hand on
his heart, his eyes gazing towards heaven. Right and
left of the flanking columns beside him kneel his wives,
Mary, née Lake, through whom Canons became a ducal
seat, and Cassandra, one of the Willoughbys of Wolla-
ton ; veiled and devout they kneel with bent heads,
like figures of Martha and Mary in the presence of the
Lord, towards whom the Duke too gazes upwards.
Chandos himself ordered the work : " *Exiguum magni
Amoris Monumentum hoc tibi statuo,*" says the inscription
touchingly, "*tui semper tuarum virtutum memor.*"[1] This
of the first wife, dead in 1712 ; Cassandra died in
1735, the Duke himself, Pope's " gracious Chandos," as
well as his too-famous Timon, in 1744, and lies " in

---

[1] " I ordain this marble to thee, the little monument of a great love ;
mindful always of thee and of thy virtues."

Hope of a Joyfull Resurrection," under the masterpiece
of his protégé the sculptor André Carpentier, neglected
by the thousands who visit the apocryphal grave of
the Harmonious Blacksmith in the churchyard
without (Plate XXVIII).

Is the work then mere display ? Surely not. The
Duke's thoughts are in heaven, as his gesture shows ;
the inscription is as modest as it is pathetic ; it is only
the artistic idiom which perplexes us. Such per-
plexities it is the object of this little book to do away
as far as may be. For all its pomp, this monument
too is one of love and grief.

Now and again history or tradition will alone explain
the character of a monument. The strange rococo
figure of Sir Robert Holmes at Yarmouth, Isle of
Wight, is so strangely at variance with the rich classical
setting typical of English works of the period that we
must turn to the records, themselves not quite consistent, if we are to understand it. The version of the
story related by the Rev. Thomas Pocock in 1704 tells
how Sir Robert, Governor of the Island from 1667 till
his death in 1692, captured a block of marble " going
to France, and the ship, being cast away on the back
of the isle, was made wreck, and belonged to this
gentleman [treasure trove being an official perquisite],
who prepared all things for his funeral and this monument, before his death." A second and more dramatic
version has it that the statue, an effigy of Louis XIV
on its way to France, was captured by Holmes on board
a French ship, together with the sculptor engaged upon
it, whom Holmes is said to have compelled to substitute his own head for that of the Grand Monarque.
Finally, we have certain undoubted facts. Holmes
left £300 in his will for the erection of the monument ;
the original inscription quoted in full by Pocock in
1704 was early removed and the present one substituted ;
and this second inscription states that the monument
was erected by Henry Holmes in memory of his honoured
uncle. How then did Pocock get hold of the tale that

the marble was treasure trove, and describe Holmes's
elaborate preparations for his own end, within eight
years of Holmes's death ; how did the second and more
picturesque account arise at all ? ; and how could the
nephew come to make his statement in a conspicuous
place on the revised inscription, under the very nose
of Holmes's friends and neighbours in a small com-
munity ?   The probability is that there is some measure
of truth in both the stories.   If Holmes got hold of a
statue either by capture or as treasure trove, and took
its sculptor prisoner, he may well have used his opportunity to get a portrait of himself, have arranged that
the resulting statue should be placed in the church
after his death (Pocock, be it observed, only says that
he " prepared all things for this monument," not that
he erected it), and have left £300 for the purpose.
That sum would have covered the elaborate Ionic
shrine in which it is set, and the nephew, who had to
make arrangements for carrying out his uncle's wishes,
would have been justified in his statement, since he
would be responsible for the architectural setting.   The
character of the statue, most emphatically un-English,
may well be due to a French sculptor, whereas
the accessories, which may be paralleled upon a
hundred English monuments, suggest the work of
Rysbrack, to whom the whole is sometimes attributed.

In the case of monuments of historical interest, a
knowledge of history is of course essential to their
understanding ; it is less easy for us, with the Oxford
Movement behind us, to understand the temper of an
age in which the sporting exploits of the dead are
cheerfully commemorated.   Yet when a battle-scene
was looked on as a fitting ornament for a tomb, we may
expect to find examples of the eccentric in sepulchral
art which it would be most unfair to judge by modern
standards.   Perhaps the extreme form of eccentricity
is reached by the double-arched monument of Sir
Thomas Parkyns at Bunny, set in the church he built,

with its inscription *Artificis status ipse fuit.*[1] The work, said to have been executed by his chaplain in a barn under his own directions, represents Parkyns, patron and representative of wrestlers, in coat and nightcap, squaring his fists for the attack ; the second arch enshrines a figure of Time, looking down on Parkyns in his coffin : the wrestler has fallen in his last bout. Art can show no more signal example of the ruling passion strong in death, and the clergy of the day protested against its erection in the chancel— a judgment against which Parkyns in his turn appealed by dwelling on its moral tendency in the third edition of his book on wrestling.

The growth of the romantic movement in literature has been often noticed. The sense of tears in mortal things is strong in Gray's *Elegy* ; the element of senti- mental tenderness, the pleasure that's all but pain, in Gilbert's words, excited the readers of Sterne. We may expect therefore to find something of the sort in monumental art, and it is there. The tender mourning women whom Roubiliac depicted, seated beside the portrait of their dead,[2] are the link between the artistic realism of the first half of the eighteenth century and the sentiment of the second.

To enter the glorious church of Halesowen in the dusk of a March evening, when the sunset lingers on the glowing sandstone, to gaze up at the soaring arches of the tower, open on three sides into the nave and aisles, to note the vistas down the aisles themselves,

---

[1] I only know this work from photographs, and should like to acknow- ledge my debt to the Rev. A. A. Kahn, Vicar of Bunny.

[2] They may be seen at Warkton, Southwick, and Walton-on-Thames. I have heard of a monument—my informant, who had seen it, unhappily could not tell me where it is, save that it is somewhere on the Kent or Sussex border—on which a seat was made by the husband's will for his living wife to sit on and lament him, a direction which, however much in harmony with the romantic fiction of the eighteenth century, is, like that fiction, something ludicrous to-day. But that it was romance, the romance of the age of hermitage and grotto, there is no doubt at all, for the influences which affected our prose and landscape gardening, and produced our countless pictures of Poor Maria, our Dodsley's Poets, and the Hermitages of our larger gardens could hardly fail to affect sepulchral art.

is an overwhelming experience after the agglomeration of mean streets outside, which, to one who knows the place only through Shenstone's eyes, are disappointment and disgust.   Within are two notable things, one the plain and frankly ugly urn bearing Shenstone's name, the other the monument of his successor at the Leasowes, Major Halliday.   Against a vast pyramid, set on great marble monoliths of Greek design wrought to represent the entrance to a vault, stand two figures separated by a column surmounted by graceful urns.   The man, in flowing robes, veils his averted face with a gesture of passionate grief, and stretches out the other hand across the barrier towards a delicate girlish figure in the dress of the day who, overcome with sorrow, kneels with clasped hands and bowed head beside the dividing column.   At her feet is curled, in all the unthinking comfort of the petted animal, a little shaggy dog.   The history of this most moving monument is as pitiful as the work is grand.   Major Halliday was a great swimmer, and was boating one June day upon the lake with his young wife when their little dog—a shag dog, as the age called any rough, long-coated beast—jumped over-board.   His heavy coat becoming soaked, he began to sink ; his master, seeing his danger, sprang out and swam to him, and seizing him struck out for the boat. Even as he held the dog up to his wife he was seized with cramp and sank before her eyes, his hands still raised above his head.

It is as if the ancient sense of the finality of death had inspired the Hellenist Banks to use his classic forms to portray not serenity but despair ; the work is essentially romantic, not in the story only but in the treatment.   Love and death are its essence and its theme, and they are none the less intense for the memory of the Greek painter whose Agamemnon veiled his face that he might not look upon his daughter's death.

How the loss of the key to the artist's meaning may lead to misunderstandings and absurd interpretations

MONUMENT OF SIR JOHN DENHAM, FATHER OF THE POET, EGHAM.
THIS VISION OF THE RESURRECTION AS A DELIVERANCE FROM
PHYSICAL DECAY IS CHARACTERISTIC OF THE EARLIER SEVEN-
TEENTH CENTURY.

PLATE XXVII.

facing p. 110.

MONUMENT OF JAMES, DUKE OF CHANDOS (POPE'S TIMON),
WHITCHURCH.   BY ANDRÉ CARPENTIER.

PLATE XXVIII.

facing p. 111.

is best explained by example.   One of the most famous witch trials of the sixteenth century was concerned with the three poor women apprehended for their sinister practices against the children of the sixth Earl of Rutland.[1]   Two of them were actually executed, and the fact that the effigies of these children are represented holding skulls upon their parents' tomb at Bottesford has been supposed to allude to their early death at the hands of these witches.   The skull, however, is part of the artistic *lingua franca* of the day, and has no more significance here than at Mayfield, for example, where an Aynscombe who was Reader at the Inner Temple and his wife have a species of halo with skulls in relief above their heads, or than beside the children of Sackville, Earl of Dorset, at Withyham, or in a hundred other cases that might be mentioned.

So too the tale of poor Bess Russell at Westminster Abbey was based on sheer ignorance of the imagery of the past.   She sits, the earliest figure in the Abbey to escape from the recumbent posture of tradition, her finger pointing to a skull at her feet.   She died of working on a Sunday, said the vergers of old ; she pricked her finger and poisoned it, and there she sits for a warning to posterity, a " martyr to good huswifery," according to Sir Roger de Coverley, who enjoyed his conductor's stories so much that " he shook him by the hand at parting, telling him that he should be very glad to see him at his lodgings in Norfolk-buildings, and talk over these matters with him more at leisure." Poor Maid of Honour, seated in her basket-chair at the wish of the sister to whom we owe her monument, to be pilloried for two centuries as a Sabbath-breaker because her sculptor placed a skull beside her to show that her living image was in truth a memory of the past !

Curiously close is the parallel of the daughter of Sir Robert Drury of Hawstead, who, tradition said, was

[1] Plate XX, *Art Journal*, 1903, p. 337.

intended to marry Henry, Prince of Wales, She died
in 1610 at the age of fifteen, and is represented both
in a portrait and on her monument at Hawstead as
resting her head on her hand. Local tradition has it
that she died of a box on the ear received from her
father.[1]

Sometimes it is the costume, not the accessories,
which is a stumbling-block. Thus the effigy of Sir John
Crewe (*ob.* 1695) at Tarporley, Cheshire, in his flowing
wig and loose robes, attended by two mourning cherubs,
was said by local tradition in 1922 to represent a lady
dead of twins in childbirth and famous in life for her
beautiful hair : Dr. Johnson himself might have been
convinced that an English epitaph were better than
a Latin, if only to avoid such vulgar errors. The
same tradition added that little Mary Knightley (p. 82),
the babe of thirteen months holding her flowers,
slipped into the well by which she gathered them
and was drowned ; they are in fact the fitting and
familiar emblem of many little maidens untimely lost.

The very charming little monument to Lord Chief
Justice William Spencer-Cowper, the poet's grandfather, at Hertingfordbury, represents him seated in
the act of delivering judgment, with two charming
girlish figures, Pallas and Prudence, to right and left
of his chair.[2] They are very pretty, very delicate, and
suggest, like so many of Roubiliac's allegorical figures,
studies from life ; but that they represent Cowper's
two wives, as one guide-book asserts, is perfectly
incredible. The monument was erected in 1754,
thirty-one years after his death ; he married his first
wife in 1688, his second wife in 1706 ; and when it was
erected his second son was Dean of Durham. For a
Dean's mother to be represented as a young girl in
transparent draperies is surely unthinkable at any time ;
yet, fortified by the authority of the guide-book,
visitors still depart with the idea that they have seen

[1] *Poems of John Donne*, ed. E. K. Chambers, ii, p. 235.
[2] Plate XI.

a portrait of the grandmother of the author of " John Gilpin." [1]

When Sir Edgar Boehm sculptured the fine monument of Lord Cardigan of the Charge of the Light Brigade at Deene in 1867, he little thought his scheme, that of the Countess leaning on her elbow and gazing at the noble recumbent figure at her side, would give rise to a legend within four years of the lady's death in 1915. Yet the local story has it that in her will she ordered her eyes to be closed when she too should die ; the eyes remain open, and the Countess haunts, and will haunt, the path outside the church until her wishes are fulfilled. It is nothing that to close her eyes were to reduce the whole design to absurdity. Open eyes are incompatible with death ; therefore they must and should be shut. Yet the same chapel contains other monuments with open eyes, and the closed eye is rare indeed on monuments ; it is only the fact that the dress is modern and the lady known to almost all the village which has created this strange modern belief as to the unsuitability of naturalism to sepulchral art.

Tradition has it too that the monument of a lady in Jamaica, by John Bacon, R.A., shows a stain of reddish marble on the very spot in which, during a negro rising, she was struck dead by a slave. I have not seen the original, and cannot say either whether the lady was so struck nor whether the flaw exists to-day ; but the belief is a clear case of *post hoc, propter hoc*. She was killed by a negro ; the flaw was there to be

---

[1] The Cowper family indeed was singularly unfortunate in the stories that arose about its members. William, the first Lord Chancellor of Great Britain, was accused by the writers of the Tory party, who hated his action in promoting the Union with Scotland, of making a mock marriage with a girl by means of a forged marriage certificate ; then—by Swift—of bigamy ; and finally, by Voltaire, of writing a treatise in favour of polygamy. His brother, the Spencer-Cowper of the monument, was actually tried—and most properly acquitted—for drowning a Quaker girl who had committed suicide, the Quakers, to save the reputation of their body, joining hands for once with the Tory party in this unscrupulous attempt to get a prominent Whig hanged.

8

accounted for ; and the sculptor in far-away London was supposed to have worked his marble so subtly as to express the lady's fate. The story even reached the sculptor's family, from whom I heard it ; the long arm of coincidence has rarely been more neatly illustrated.

Mere ignorance, however, is accountable for more than one legend of an erring sculptor expiating his offence by suicide. The little church of Ravenstone, Bucks, contains a monument to Heneage Finch, first Lord Nottingham (ob. 1682), who played an important and not wholly discreditable part in the legal proceedings during the Popish Plot and was father of the second Earl, Swift's Don Dismallo and Arbuthnot's Don Diego, the " black Daniel Finch " of his own day. The work is conceived on the lines of a four-post bed, with tester and curtains complete, under which lies the Lord Chancellor in robes and full-bottomed wig and with an undoubted squint, whether due to a personal peculiarity or an accident of the carving may be doubted. Local legend has it that the sculptor was so shocked by the discovery of the defect that he went home and killed himself. The monument, as Miss Pearl Finch informed me, is said by family tradition to be by the elder Cibber, whose hand it suggests, but, though he lived peacefully till 1700, the art of verifying dates is no part of the legend-monger's game, and the suicide story holds its ground both here and at Winchester, where it is told of Sir Henry Cheere, sculptor of the large monument to Bishop Willis (ob. 1734) on the south wall of the nave, representing him in full canonicals half-rising from the sarcophagus on which he lies at the summons of the Archangel. The position of the work involves the fact that the Bishop lies with his back to the altar, and the sculptor was so much shocked by the discovery that he went home and killed himself. " It's a queer thing," added my informant, " but the family knows nothing about it. I had the Misses Cheere here a few years back, and they were very interested." Well they might be ! Cheere lived on till 1781 and died, a baronet, full of years and honour, after a valuable career of social and magisterial work undertaken when he had ceased to be an active partner in the business which ultimately narrowed itself to the mantelpiece and leaden-figure factory over which the satirists of the age made merry. But "the Hyde Park Corner man," as Colman called him, was a very competent sculptor in a nobler medium, marble, before prosperity made him merely the head of the firm ; and Bishop Willis is a fine thing in his own kind. The fact, of course, is that the position of a monument in any cathedral depends not on the sculptor but on the Dean and Chapter ; J. T. Smith, indeed, bitterly complains that patrons ordering a monument usually gave its author no idea where it was to be placed. Therefore, if suicide came in at all, it should have been the Dean and Chapter who committed it ; but as they did not, and as the blasphemy of the westward position had to be atoned for, it is the sculptor who must pay the penalty.

But we must beware of dismissing all local stories as absurd. No better example of their value could be given than the story of the statue of Clement Spelman at Narborough, Norfolk, already more than once alluded to.[1] Tradition said that he was of so haughty a temper that he ordered his coffin to be placed upright inside the pedestal : in his life he had never been trodden on ; he would not be trodden on after his death. When the church was restored in 1865 the coffin was found upright inside the eight-foot pedestal, which was cut down by half and the coffin reburied, by a cruel stroke of irony, in the north-west angle of the nave, under the seats assigned to the Sunday-school children, whose feet thus tread upon the man twice pictured in this very church, once as the hoped-for heir upon his parents' tomb (p. 80), once in the handsome robes of a Recorder of Nottinghamshire.

[1] Plate IX.

A few weeks after visiting the church I was looking through the volume of Cibber drawings already alluded to when I came upon Clement Spelman's figure in its unused fantastic setting of draperies, cherub heads, and allegorical figures of Time and Death, one with his scythe and hour-glass, the other a skeleton holding a dart and wiping his eyes on the surrounding drapery. The statue, minutely and beautifully drawn, was duly reproduced without the preposterous accessories, and it is fortunate indeed that we are able to assign so rare a sepulchral form as a standing figure of Charles II's reign to a sculptor of such high distinction; fortunate that the original drawing and the completed work can thus be compared; fortunate above all that the story vouched for by tradition has been thus signally vindicated.

CHAPTER XI

SOME REPRESENTATIVE SCULPTORS—I

We may well regret the obscurity which surrounds
the name of " Richard Parker the Alablaster man," [1]
to whom we owe the magnificent monument of the first
Earl of Rutland at Bottesford, with its noble effigies,
rich Renaissance detail, and remarkable isolated figure.
It cost the modest sum of £24 in 1544, and its author
must be reckoned among the greatest sculptors of the
earlier English school ; but nothing is known of him,
or of one Donbins,[2] who carved the splendid tomb of
Sir Thomas Salusbury (*ob.* 1578) at Whitchurch, Denbigh, erected by his widow, which has in common with
Parker's work a series of realistic and exquisite little
figures on the base facing instead of in profile, and
divided by elaborate pilasters, not by a continuous frieze.

Gerard or *Garet Johnson* or *Janssen*, on the other
hand, has become, since the publication of the Bottesford documents by Lady Victoria Manners in 1903,
much more than a lay figure. He was born in Holland,
came to England about 1567, settled down in Southwark, married an English wife Mary, and had a large
family, of whom several sons, Bernard, John, Nicholas,
and the younger Gerard—world-famous as the sculptor
of Shakespeare's monument—followed his profession.
He was invited by the Rutland family to Bottesford
and commissioned to execute the monuments of the
third and fourth Earls of Rutland, who died within a
year of each other, his son Nicholas himself doing that

---

[1] *Art Journal*, 1903, pp. 272 ff.
[2] W. M. Myddelton, *Pedigree of the Family of Myddelton of Gwaynynog*,
1910, p. 84 ; *A.M.C. Denbighshire*, p. 43. I do not understand the de-
preciation of the work there expressed, as the details are of the utmost
refinement and delicacy.

of the fifth Earl, and in the Household Accounts of the family we read a good deal about him. His son came down to help him in the erection of the monuments, which were sent by sea to Boston and thence, in carts drawn by sixteen oxen, to the church ; there was a good deal of trouble over the men's lodgings and their food, the local tradesmen trying to take advantage of the strangers ; but all went well in the end, and Johnson received £200 for the two, a reasonable fee for the time, and the works were " inriched," i.e. painted and gilt, by the painter John Mathews of Nottingham in 1592. The date of Johnson's death is unknown, but the influence of his school was immense, and its products may be found all over England.[1] His sons worked in the same manner, and in several cases we are fortunate in possessing documentary evidence which enables us to trace the development of their style over a period of some sixty years.

That style is distinguished by an exquisite finish, a dignity worthy of the finest mediæval tombs, a remarkable power of achieving finished portraits both of men and women ; the designs are of the time, canopied altar-tombs with kneeling figures on the base, or mural monuments with kneeling parents and kneeling children appendant or forming a frieze below, framed by delicate panels of ribbon work and wreaths often supporting emblems of mortality. The background and supporting slab are usually of touch, the figures and decorative panels of alabaster. The gadroon or edging pattern 0⁰0⁰0 or 0∘0∘0 may be taken as a hall-mark of the Southwark workshops ; so too the use of elaborate coats-of-arms upon the cornice, often with obelisks between, though there is a subtle difference between such escutcheons and the very similar ones beloved of Cure : the Johnsons tend to rounded strap-work decoration, the Cures to those whose outer curves

[1] Examples are, I suggest: (1) in sandstone, that of Sir Thomas Offley at St. Andrew Undershaft ; (2) in alabaster, that of Justice Shallow himself, grandfather of the Sir Thomas Lucy of the Schurman monument, at Charlcote, erected by Shallow in 1595–6, when his wife died.

suggest the lines of a cow's horn. Gerard's son *Nicholas*, author of the magnificent tomb of the fifth Earl of Rutland already mentioned, uses small allegorical figures on the cornice as well as obelisks and coats-of-arms and a winged death's head surmounted by an hour-glass, a detail which, as it occurs only on monuments closely resembling that of the Earl, may be taken as a hall-mark of his workshop. Such accessible monuments as those of Lady Dacre in Chelsea Old Church [1] or the Kinloss family in the Museum of the Record Office, once in the Chapel of the Rolls, may profitably be compared with the Bottesford monument and are obviously the work of the same hand.

The allegorical figures on the Bottesford monument are repeated on the Shakespeare monument by Nicholas's brother Gerard and elsewhere ; were the idioms of English sculpture better understood, we should have been spared much nonsense on the supposed esoteric meaning of these symbolic *amorini*, asleep and holding a spade, personifying Labour and Rest.

Yet another trick, repeated over and over in the seventy odd monuments I have noted as belonging to the Johnson studio, is to draw the cloak of a re-cumbent female figure across the right knee in vigorous folds ; and the use of gold and colour, not indiscriminate but finely applied, is almost universal. It is one more proof of the close association between sculpture and architecture that yet another Johnson, Bernard, was responsible for the carrying out the designs of North-umberland House and Audley End, as well as for carving the tomb of Sir Nicholas and Lady Bacon at Redgrave (1620),[2] the effigies on which were the work of Nicholas Stone. Bernard's brother Nicholas had signed the agreement relating to the Sutton monument in the Charterhouse before his junior Nicholas Stone,[3]

---

[1] Lady Dacre's monument is described in an article in *The Times* of February 4, 1927 ; the artistic affinities of the work are, however, not dealt with. Another very fine and characteristic work is Sir John Spencer's tomb in St. Helen's, Bishopsgate.

[2] Walpole Society, vii, p. 52.   [3] *Ibid.*, p. 40.

and we have further evidence of collaboration between the Johnsons and the head of another Southwark studio in the agreement for the Montague monument signed by Johnson and Cure (p. 123).

John Johnson or *Jan Janson*, as he signs himself, yet another brother, signed on June 20, 1624, an agreement with Paul d'Ewes for the fine monument at Stowlangtoft, Suffolk, whose terms are illuminating.[1] " Jan Janson of the [parish of] St. Martin-in-the-Fields in the County of Midd., Stone cutter," covenants to make " seven pictures kneeling, a full yard high, graven and coloured to the life." " The Tombe or Monument of the best alablaster, touch, black marble, rance &c," the figures to be of " a boy of foure years old, kneeling, and two others being dead, and a maide of ten yeares old," " a boy of two yeares old, and foure pictures more of women on the other side ; " of the principal figures " the man to be in a gowne, the women wite [*sic*] veiled." The eldest daughter, a married woman, is to have her arms shown, " the two others [are] maidens of eighteen years, the fourthe a child of seaven yeares." The work was to be finished by August 24 at the trifling cost of £16 10*s.*, though its height was to be eight feet and its breadth six ; the two main pillars and the space for the epitaph are duly specified, " according to a plott made and drawne and shewed to the said Paule dewes before."

That such care was bestowed on so cheap a work explains both the fine quality of these monuments with kneeling figures and the extraordinary number extant.

Later works of the Johnson school, such as the Aynscombe monument at Mayfield (after 1633), show the influence of the movement towards a looser composition and freer drapery, and may profitably be compared with Stone's later work ; but of the Johnson school in its earlier stages it may safely be said that the style is so well marked as to make the identification of works

---

[1] This agreement (Harl. MSS. 98, 20, verso 21*) has not hitherto been quoted, owing probably to a wrong reference in the *D.N.B.*

from their studio at once certain and delightful, and the elder Gerard and his son Nicholas at least must be placed among the greatest of English sculptors, as beyond doubt also they are our first sculptor-archæologists. The singular series of monuments to the Poyntz family at North Ockendon, Essex, commemorating its members from the fifteenth to the seventeenth centuries, with their valiant efforts at correctness of costume, are still unparalleled ; they are obviously the work of the Johnson who carved the Sir Gabriel Poyntz (*ob.* 1607) in the same church, by whom this singular series of ancestors was erected.[1]

There is no documentary evidence to prove that *Richard Stephens*, painter, medallist, and sculptor, was connected with the Johnsons, but his splendid monument to Robert Radcliffe, Earl of Sussex, at Boreham, Essex, shows such marks of the Southwark school as to suggest that they worked together. The gadroon or dot-and-dash ornament already noted, the types of ribbon work and emblematic decoration round the heraldic shields, and identical with those on known works of the Johnson school, and the recumbent effigies are wholly in their manner. Lord Sussex himself ordered the erection of the work, and Vertue fortunately preserves the details of the agreement, which he saw among the papers of Peter Le Neve, Norroy herald (*cf.* Chapter I). As the Earl left £1,500 for his funeral and monument, it will be seen that the sculptor's share, £292 12s. 8d. was a small one.[2]

Cornelius Cure or *Cuer* (*ob.* 1607) was born in the

---

[1] Walpole Society, vii, p. 41. The article " Gerard Johnson " in the *D.N.B.* is of real value for the study of the subject, but does not adequately distinguish the work of the various members of the family, and was written before the Bottesford documents were known.

[2] B.M. Add. MSS. 23072, f. 35a. Vertue adds that Sussex's executor Sir Christopher Wray was responsible for the arrangements. The More tomb at Guildford is so like the Sussex that it is probably the work of Stephens. It may be well to add that the touch referred to in this agreement and elsewhere was a kind of black marble quite distinct from the black statuary marble sometimes specified. Rance, a material mentioned in the Johnson agreements, is a native red marble.

parish of St. Thomas the Apostle, Southwark, and the fact makes it probable that he was a son of Thomas Cure (*ob*. 1588), saddler to Edward VI, Mary, and Elizabeth, M.P. for Southwark in the first, thirteenth, and twenty-seventh years of Queen Elizabeth, and founder of a Southwark almshouse, whose plain altar-tomb is in St. Saviour's, Southwark.[1] The family may have been of Flemish descent, since one William Cure, who made " the clay figure of the Tartar, lately brought to England by Sir Martin Frobisher," [2] was " a Ducheman graver." Cornelius also is mentioned by Meres in *Palladis Tamia* as an excellent engraver, was Master Mason to Elizabeth and James I, and was responsible for the design of the " two stately tombs at Westminster, one for the Queen Elizabeth, another for his Majesty's mother," Mary, Queen of Scots,[3] which at his death in 1607 were completed by his son, who received £865 10*s*. for his share in the works—the elaborate settings presumably, since, as we shall see, Colt was certainly responsible for the figure of Queen Elizabeth. Cornelius Cure was buried in the church of St. Thomas the Apostle, and his studio passed to his son—

William Cure (*ob*. 1632), who succeeded his father as Master Mason to the King, and began his independent career by working on the unfinished Royal tombs [4] in Westminster Abbey. On January 4, 1610–11, he signed an agreement [5] with Sir Roger Aston of Cranford, Middlesex, in which he is described as " William Cure,

---

[1] My son suggested the relationship to Cornelius ; an account of the tomb will be found in Britton and Brayley's *Surrey*, v (1850), p. 365.

[2] I take this from the *D.N.B.*, together with the reference to Meres.

[3] Lascelles to Lord Shrewsbury, letter quoted in Lodge's *Illustrations of British History*, iii (1838), p. 145.

[4] The final painting was the work of one James Mauncey or Manutie. The total cost of these great monuments, according to an Office Book in the Harleian Collection, was £3,500, a sum unparalleled for English monuments at any period, if the value of money is taken into account. BM. Lansdowne MSS. 164 also has notes of payment.

[5] *Gentleman's Magazine*, 1800, lxx, p. 105. The monument is engraved in Lysons's *Middlesex*, 1800, *s.v.* " Cranford." The poetical names of Sir Roger's wives, Mary Stuart and Cordelia Stanhope, are hardly more charming than their forms.

esq. of St. Thomas the Apostle in Southwark," to make
a monument to Sir Roger, Master of the King's Great
Wardrobe, " well and sufficiently and workmanlike,
to the best of his power, art and carving," of " alabaster,
tuche, rance, and white and black marble," with " the
seven pictures [of Sir Roger, his wives and their four
daughters] to be kneeling upon the same," a fifth daughter, dead in early youth, being in fact added lying at
her father's side.   The " pattern " of the work having
been " subscribed with Sir Roger Aston and William
Cure," it was to be " set up, placed, fully finished, painted
and guilden, in the parish church of Cranforth att, or
before, April 30, 1613," at a cost of £180.

On November 25, 1618, an agreement was signed
between " Sir Charles Montague of London, Knight, on
the one parte, and William Cuer, citizen and free mason
of London, and Nicholas Johnson, of the parish of
St. Savio^r in Southwark, in the countie of Surrie, carver,
on the other," to set up a monument to Bishop Montague of Winchester in Bath Abbey, " according to one
plate thereof drawne and by the said William and
Nicholas allreadie delivered to the said Sr Charles Montague," " to be saffelie conveyed to the said citie of
Bath and there erected." [1] This work, now sadly
mutilated, was fortunately twice drawn by Dingley (Pls.
XIX, XXIX,[2] and showed the prelate in Garter robes
recumbent on an altar-tomb with two great Corinthian
columns joined by architraves loaded with heraldic
devices at his head and feet. It is only from this
agreement that we know of Cure's association with the
Johnson studio, whose products bear so marked a resemblance to his own.[3]   He worked under Inigo Jones
at Whitehall, and on August 4, 1632, was buried in

[1] T. Dingley, *History from Monuments*, Camden Society, 1867–8, vol. ii,
p. 155.   The tomb cost £200.
[2] Vol. i, as above.
[3] It is one of the misfortunes of divided authorship that the article on
the Johnsons in the *D.N.B.* contains no allusion to his alliance with Cure,
and that Johnson is ignored in the Life of Cure, in the same work of
reference.   The Cotton monument at Landwade (Plate XXII) is a fine
and little known example of the school.

his parish church, his successor as Master Mason being Nicholas Stone.

Maximilian Colt or Coulte, formerly Poultrain, Poutrain, or Powtran (fl. 1600–41), is said to have been a Huguenot born at Arras who came to England towards the end of the sixteenth century.   On March 4, 1604–5, he signed an agreement with Lord Treasurer Cecil "to carve the monument above Queen Elizabeth's grave" for £500 [1]; that effigy therefore is his work. By a warrant dated March 17, 1606, Lord Salisbury, at the King's wish, "made a contract" for the tomb of the baby princess Sophia "with Maximilian Poutrain alias Coult," the cost not to be above £140, though he in fact received £215.[2]   On July 28, 1608, he was appointed Master Carver to the King; on March 3, 1609, was granted a suit of broadcloth and fur annually for life; between 1611 and 1624 was engaged at intervals in carving the barges of the Royal Family; in 1633 held the post of Master Sculptor to the King, at a salary of £8 a year; and in 1641 was imprisoned in the Fleet, his speedy release leading to an inquiry into the conduct of the Warden.   His alleged responsibility for the design and building of Wadham College is more than problematical.

Colt was closely connected with the parish of St. Bartholomew, Smithfield; in 1618 indeed he was living with his son John, also a sculptor, in Farringdon Ward, but he had a house in Bartholomew Close; his daughter Abigail was buried in the church on March 29, 1629, as were his son John, who was, like his father, born at Arras, and his wife Susan (*ob.* 1646).   He had also a son named Alexander.[3]

We have seen the first Lord Salisbury's name in connection with Colt; we have now to consider his own

[1] *D.N.B.* and authorities there cited.

[2] Lodge's *Illustrations of British History*, iii, p. 195.   The pretty inscription "Sophia Rosula Regia . . . praepropera fata decerpta . . . ut in Christi Rosario reflorescat," deserves to be better known.

[3] These statements are taken from the *D.B.N.*, Walpole's *Anecdotes*, and Lodge's *Illustrations*.

monument by that sculptor, hitherto ascribed to Simon Basil, but as Mr. Christopher Hussey has conclusively proved,[1] in reality the work of Colt, who had already sent in a model and whose estimates Basil, the Surveyor-General, checked in a document still preserved at Hatfield.

The Earl had left £200 for the erection of a fair monument to himself at Hatfield, directing that the white staff which he bore as Lord Treasurer should be placed on the monument which his son, the second Earl, built the Salisbury Chapel to receive. On January 4, 1613–14, Basil signed a note " for the finishing of the intended tomb, according to a model thereof made for the Right Hon. the late Lord Treasurer of England " [Robert Cecil, first Earl of Salisbury], with an estimate of the workmanship and setting up :

Of white marble for the 6 figures	140 ft.
Of tuche [black touch-stone] for both the tables [slabs above and below the effigy]	70 ft.
Of Kaen [Caen stone] for enrichment	3 ft.
The charge of sawing and carving of the 6 figures, if they be done according to art and true proportion, are worth £60 a piece	£360
The two tables of tuche, with sawing, polishing and workmanship of the same	£60
The carriage of the said tomb to that field, setting of it up and finishing	£40

Sum to be	£460

SY. BASYLL.[2]

On a great slab of touchstone, supported by kneeling figures of Fortitude, Temperance, Truth, and Justice, lies his effigy, a magnificent figure, in full robes, bearing his own white staff, perhaps the only old one in existence, since the breaking of the staff on leaving office is a well-known piece of etiquette ; on the slab below is a skeleton in the same attitude. The allegorical figures are strongly Italian in character, the arrangement of

[1] *Country Life*, March 29, 1927. This and the preceding number are full of illustrations of internal woodwork at Hatfield suggestive of Colt's work in the Abbey.

[2] I take this very important document from *Some Memories of Bishops Hatfield and its Past*, by the Rev. J. J. Antrobus (2nd ed.), Hatfield, 1925.

the hair in particular suggesting the drawings of Michael
Angelo, though the recumbent figure of the Earl is
in the finest English manner. (Plate VII.)

On the strength of this monument we may safely
identify as Colt's the superb tomb of Sir Francis Vere
in the Chapel of St. John the Evangelist, Westminster
Abbey, on which that gallant hero of the Low Country
Wars, who died in his bed (whence his civilian dress)
in 1609, is depicted at rest on a great slab of touchstone
borne on the shoulders of his four kneeling sons.[1]

But, it may be asked, why call these men English
sculptors ? Because they settled in England, died in
England, and like a dozen other foreign artists are
included in the *Dictionary of National Biography*.
English-born sculptors we have in plenty, but to exclude
foreign artists, many of them men whose work is unknown outside England, were to impoverish our art to
no purpose.

Our knowledge of *Nicholas Stone* (1586–1647) is,
happily, far greater, thanks to the Walpole Society's
publication of his Note and Account Books in 1919,
so admirably edited by the late Mr. W. L. Spiers, by
means of which, in an age when the habit of signing
monuments was scarcely known, we can follow the
progress of his art from 1614 to 1647, learn the price
of his works from the simplest tablet to the most elaborate
monument, and watch the development of new sculptural motives and ideas. The only justification indeed
for treating him here is the representative character
of his work and the intimate connection between his
studio and others of the day. His interest is that he
is a transitional figure ; in his earliest works not going
beyond the conceptions of his predecessors, but always
experimenting, and in his cherubs and broken pediments
which dominate our mural monuments down to 1800,
as in the innovation of contemporary portraits in

---

[1] There is a curious late seventeenth century tomb of the same type at
Dalton Holme, Yorkshire, which must be a direct imitation of the Salisbury
monument, skeleton and all.   I have to thank the Rector for much information as to this interesting work, which I know only from photographs.

classical armour, we can trace many of the ideas characteristic of later monumental sculpture.

Stone's father was a quarryman (perhaps a journey-
man mason) at Woodbury, near Exeter, where the
sculptor was baptised on July 21, 1587. In 1606 he
was in London, where he met Hendrik de Keyser, who
was in England for the purpose of studying the Royal
Exchange with a view to his own future work at Amsterdam, to which city he was sculptor and master mason.
De Keyser persuaded Stone to return as his pupil,
and in Amsterdam he fell in love with his master's
daughter Maria and married her on April 25, 1613,
in which year he returned to London and took the
premises in Long Acre which he occupied until his death.

From that time onwards we can follow his work in
detail down to the outbreak of the Civil War. It is
needless to do more than say that his works may be
found from Westminster Abbey to Holyrood, from
Yorkshire to Kent, that they range from the font at
Stanmore to the famous porch of St. Mary's, Oxford,
from great monuments like those of the founder of the
Charterhouse and the Villiers tomb in the Abbey to
simple and exquisite tablets like those to Ben Jonson's
" son " Randolph the dramatist at Blatherwick and
such elaborate busts as that of Sir Thomas Bodley in
Merton Chapel. Stone died on September 17, 1647,
and was buried in old St. Martin's-in-the-Fields. He
left an artist son Henry, the " Old Stone " best known
as a copyist of Vandyke ; a son Nicholas, also a sculptor,
who survived his father only a month, and whose diary
of his foreign tour, now in the British Museum, is of
high interest, since it records his meetings with Bernini ;
and yet another, John, later Cibber's master, some of
whose work is fortunately known. He had, as we shall
see, several assistants, among them two sons of de
Keyser, whose share in some of his monuments is
recorded ; and his great-nephew Charles Stoakes, from
whom Vertue learnt many interesting facts about the
sculptors of the next generation, inherited his business

and the precious note-books, four of which ultimately came into the hands of Sir John Soane, and are among the greatest treasures of the Soane Museum in Lincoln's Inn Fields.

One of Stone's assistants, *John Schurman* or *Schoerman*, " born at Emden in the Low Countries," is known from Vertue's having extracted from two of his account books all the information we possess.[1] He worked on Sir Simon Baskerville's monument, for "Sir John Danvers of Chelsey," for whom he made statues of Hercules and Antæus, two shepherds, and " a Spinks of Portland stone," besides the " arms &c. of Lord Spencer, his tomb," [2] the work of N. Stone, Junior, " the " Statue of the Lord Belhaven lying on a side of white marble " and " the Little Boy " for the same nobleman's tomb at Holyrood, and " the Statue lying on a side representing Sr Thomas Lucy of Warwickshire white marble," which has been rashly attributed to Bernini, for which he received £18, besides £2 10s. for " polishing and glasing." The Belhaven tomb I have not seen, but the magnificent effigy of Sir Thomas Lucy already mentioned (p. 58) places Schoerman high among our sculptors. The bas-relief of Lucy riding in Charlcote Chase (p. 87) is not specified in Vertue's extracts, but we are probably justified in ascribing it to the same hand.

Of a far more famous man, *Caius Gabriel Cibber*, we have at last (1926) a satisfactory biography,[3] though it omits his work at Belvoir and Bottesford and the volume of drawings here so often quoted.

Cibber was a Dane by birth, the son of the cabinet-maker to the King of Denmark, who, on discovering the youth's talent, sent him to Rome at his own expense. He came to England " a year or thereabouts before the Restoration," [4] and became foreman to Stone, whom he brought home from a visit to Holland when that sculptor

[1] B.M. Add. MSS. 23,069, f. 15b.

[2] B.M. Add. MSS. 23,073, f. 9b.

[3] *The Life and Works of Caius Gabriel Cibber*, by Harald Faber (Oxford, 1926).

[4] As Charles Stoakes, who knew him, told Vertue.

had a stroke. After his death in 1667 Cibber set up
for himself, became Carver to the King's Closet, and
soon had a handsome practice. His patrons included
the first Duke of Devonshire and Lord Rutland, and
much work of his is still to be found at Chatsworth and
Bottesford, where he executed the monuments of the
seventh and eighth Earls of Rutland.[1] He worked at
Hampton Court under Wren ; married twice, his
second wife being a Rutlandshire heiress whom he must
have met at Bottesford and by whom he had several
children, of whom Colley Cibber, dramatist, *causeur*,
and enemy of Pope, was the eldest. In his earlier life
he was led into gambling and suffered imprisonment
for debt, and it was as a prisoner in the King's Bench
that he " went backwards and forwards daily," as
Vertue tells us, to execute the bas-relief upon the Monument.[2] Of his monuments, only the impressive tomb
at Withyham, showing Lord and Lady Dorset kneeling
on either side of the altar-tomb on which their son lies
dying,[3] has been published, though that of Lord Nottingham (p. 114) is a striking work which confirms the
family tradition ascribing it to him ; but entirely new
light is thrown upon the subject by the unpublished
Notebook, which reveals him as the unsuspected author
of a number of important tombs and monumental

[1] An interesting letter from him on the subject is given in the *Art Journal*
for 1903, p. 325.

[2] His most imaginative works are the figures of Raving and Melancholy
Madness, executed for the gates of Bedlam, the former one a portrait of
Oliver Cromwell's porter, himself a maniac there. Maltreated as they
have been, these figures, now in the Guildhall Museum, are the strongest
ideal subjects of their age, if only in their perception of the tragedy of
madness in an age when it was a mockery and a show.

[3] Plate X ; Faber's *Cibber*, pl. vii. The work produced a great effect
upon a Sussex schoolmaster in 1749, who called it " an incomparable
fine monument, erected to the former Duke and Dutchess and their 13
children ; the surviving children are represented as holding an olive-
branch in their hands, those deceased a death's head. On the north side
of this monument kneels the Duke in his armour, and a commanding-
staff in his right hand. On the south side the Dutchess, in her boddice
and a dress used in those times ; and on the top their eldest son, lying
nearly supine, with a skull held on his left knee, and resting himself on his
elbow " (" Journal of Walter Gale," *Sussex Arch. Coll.*, ix, p. 199)

9

tablets not hitherto associated with any studio. Among
the former may be named the fine Dame Dorothy
Brownlowe at Sutton, hidden now behind the organ,
the Spelman statue at Narborough, the Sir William
Russell at St. Dunstan's-in-the-East, designed but not
erected in his lifetime, the Mrs. Mary Brownlow,
executed like the Spelman without the attendant
figures, at St. Lawrence Jewry.

His work at Bottesford consists of two monuments :
one, that of the seventh Earl, a clumsy imitation of
Bushnell ; one, of the eighth Earl, enabling us to identify
as his a familiar type of monument with standing figures
in semi-classical dress,[1] neither represented in the book
of drawings, and therefore of especial interest. Many
of the finest drawings, notably those with busts, still
await identification ; but after the discoveries already
made there is little doubt that most, if not all, actually
exist, and publication would doubtless lead to the
discovery of the monuments themselves. His grotesque
allegories excepted, he exemplifies all the tendencies
of the day. He gives us reclining figures, standing
figures, busts, mural tablets, even altar-tombs ; his
mural monuments show a free use of the cherub, the
hanging curtain, the medallion, and the swag, and a
freedom of line which is positively rococo ; and he
revels, as we have seen, in the *macabre*. It is hardly
too much to say that he is revealed by the Notebook
as one of the most important figures in our sculpture
between Stone and Rysbrack.

The drawings further prove that Cibber's studio was
in existence for a year or two at least after his death,
since his designs were in the hands of his successors
when Sir William Russell died two years after the
sculptor, and his monument is, very significantly,
reversed from the drawing.[2] Many tablets and mural
monuments of the next half-century are so similar

---

[1] *Art Journal*, p. 269. The monument of Sir William Maynard at Little
Easton, Essex, much resembles the Bottesford tomb.

[2] The inscription proves it was not erected in Sir William's lifetime.

in character to the drawings that it would seem as if they had come from an *atelier* in which the Cibber tradition was familiar ; who were his successors there is no evidence to show, nor is anything known of his assistants.

For convenience' sake Cibber has been treated with the Stones, but his rival the English *John Bushnell* was probably the older man.   An apprentice of Thomas Burman, himself an apprentice of Stone, Bushnell was entrapped by his master into an unsuitable marriage ; bolted to the Continent with £15 belonging to him when sent to the country to supervise the erection of a monument ;   and worked his way across Europe, working in Flanders, France, and Italy, and eventually finding a home in Venice, where he stayed some years and erected a vast monument to a Venetian Procurator representing a victory of the Venetian fleet over the Turks off Candia.   He returned to England not long after the Restoration at the suggestion of an English nobleman, was received by Charles II, found plenty of patrons, and was commissioned to execute several statues of that sovereign, one of which still survives, along with the companion figure of Charles I, in the uncongenial precincts of the Old Bailey.[1]

Bushnell's monuments are numerous and interesting. His dramatic genius finds its fullest expression in such works as the Mordaunt monument at Fulham (Plate VIII) and the wonderful figure of William Ashburnham, kneeling with hands outstretched towards his dying wife, whom cherubs beckon to the skies ; but he is a very unequal master, and his art cannot be dismissed under any single formula.   At its best, it is among the finest English baroque in existence ; at its worst it is both clumsy and irritating.   But he had a great gift of dramatic design, and his work is never quite negligible.   Haughty, passionate, and unhappy, he lost his estate in a lawsuit ;

---

[1] They were identified and published in the *Architect* in 1922 ; *cf. The Times,* May 17, 1925.   For a full account of Bushnell see the volume of the Walpole Society for 1926–7.

his ambitious Trojan Horse, a colossal structure in whose head twelve men could sit at table, was wrecked in a gale ; and he died, poor and mad, in 1701, to be buried at Paddington, where the Registers containing the entry relating to his burial are missing.

Grinling Gibbons (1648–1721),[1] best known for his incomparable woodwork, was also responsible for much work both in bronze and marble. Of parentage half-English and half-Dutch, he spent his youth in Holland, came to England as a young man, and worked in York-shire before coming to London, where Betterton the actor employed him on some carving for the Duke of York's Play-house. This work struck Lely the painter. He made inquiries, and, like Evelyn (who, as the oft-repeated story in his Diary tells us, found him working on a carving from Tintoretto's Crucifixion), recommended him to Charles II. It was a fortunate moment for sculptors. The Fire had opened the way for work under Wren ; the increasing luxury of the Court, which aimed at emulating that of Louis XIV, led to the adornment of some palaces and the building or enlargement of others, as well as to the erection of new houses for the greater nobles. All over England—at Windsor, Hampton Court, Petworth, Chatsworth, Stowe, and a score of other great houses—Gibbons's hand is to be found, and Wren's fortunate admiration for his work is proved by St. Paul's and the City churches. Gibbons's statues cannot be touched on here, but his authorship of a series of monuments up and down the country is less commonly realised.   That of Mrs. Beaufoy in Westminster Abbey is the most accessible, but at Con-ington,[2] Fulham, St. Mary Abbots (though the Courten monument is a mere wreck to-day), Ashstead, Hare-

[1] Mr. Avray Tipping's splendid monograph is indispensable to a study of the sculptor, but on the monumental side his work is not fully treated.

[2] It is remarkable that this little monument, discussed in Chapter VII, appears to be the only work with the sculptor's signature *G. Gibbons fec*. Mrs. Beaufoy is stated on the base to be by " Mr. Gibbons " and is not properly speaking signed at all. The others here mentioned are known to be by him from documentary evidence alone.

TIME CARRYING OFF THE CHILDREN OF SHEFFIELD, DUKE
OF BUCKINGHAM, WESTMINSTER ABBEY. ALLEGORICAL
FIGURE BY DELVAUX SURMOUNTING SCHEEMAKER'S
EFFIGIES OF THE DUKE IN ROMAN DRESS AND THE
DUCHESS IN CONTEMPORARY COSTUME.

PLATE XXIX.

facing p. 132.

MONUMENT TO THOMAS GUY, IN CHAPEL OF GUY'S HOSPITAL. BY JOHN BACON, R.A. A FINE WORK, CHARACTERISTIC OF THE HUMANE AGE OF JOHN HOWARD AND JONAS HANWAY.

PLATE XXXI.

MONUMENT OF DR. HUGO CHAMBERLEN, WESTMINSTER ABBEY. BY PETER SCHEEMAKER. THE DOCTOR, IN THE GOWN OF THE ROYAL COLLEGE OF PHYSICIANS IS ATTENDED BY FIGURES OF HYGIEIA, AND GRATITUDE. WHILE A CHERUB ABOVE THE PYRAMID OF ETERNITY BECKONS HIM TO HEAVEN. THE INFLUENCE OF GREEK ART IN THE ALLEGORICAL FIGURES IS VERY MARKED.

field, and Exton—the latter a vast structure costing £1,000—his work may be seen and sometimes admired, though his busts, which were much thought of at the time, appear to be lost.[1] He had a large band of competent assistants, among them being the most notable sculptor of the next generation,

Francis Bird (1667–1731), who first appears as an assistant of Wren at Oxford, and may well have been the son of a local sculptor, the William Byrd who signs the Fettiplace monuments at Swinbrook,[2] since only the supposition that his father was an enthusiast for the same art can explain the fact that Francis was actually sent to Brussels to study under a sculptor of the name of Cozins before he was eleven.[3] He went to Rome to work under the great Le Gros ; stayed until he was about nineteen, by which time he had almost forgotten his mother-tongue [3] ; and on his return to England found employment with Gibbons. He executed the west pediment and the figures of the Apostles on St. Paul's for Wren, and after a second and briefer visit to Rome set up in Westminster and made a well-deserved reputation as a sculptor with the admirable monument of Dr. Busby in Westminster Abbey (Plate XIII). Its simplicity and dignity—the great headmaster is represented in his D.D. gown and cap, reclining on his elbow —make it one of the best works of its age, but the absence of a wig gives it for our generation an almost unfair advantage over other contemporary tombs. It is a melancholy fact that, after this admirable work, Bird produced one or two of the worst monuments in Westminster Abbey. Even his own age laughed at Sir Cloudesley Shovel, though there it is the figure, not the dignified setting, which is absurd ; and even the best of the others are not quite inspired, though

[1] That of Sir Peter Lely, in the Church of St. Paul, Covent Garden, was burnt in 1791.

[2] This is a new theory, but I venture to suggest that it is probably correct. The Fettiplace monuments were erected *en bloc* in 1657, and represent three generations of the family.

[3] Bird himself told Vertue these facts.

that of South has great merit, and the bust of Sidney
Godolphin is admirable. Bird indeed had far more
power than it is the fashion to allow, and the great
west pediment of St. Paul's, if not, as a contemporary
rhymester said, worthy of Phidias or Praxiteles,[1] is,
like his Apostles on the roof,[2] a very creditable composition in the baroque manner, not unbefitting the
pupil of Le Gros. But it is in the crypt of St. Paul's
that Bird's most touching work—far beyond "the
many lofty Tombs and Magnificent Monuments" commemorated in the obituary notice in the Press [3]—may
be found. This is his mural tablet to Jane Wren, the
well-beloved daughter of his colleague, Sir Christopher,
representing her as St. Cecilia. This and the Busby at
least may be termed, in the words of Bird's obituarist,
"lasting monuments of Mr. Bird's reputation and skill
to Posterity as long as Marble can last."

Bird slipped on some ice in the winter of 1729, and
was lame till his death in consequence. Almost the
only other personal facts we know about him are that
Pope wrote to him in a very cavalier fashion about the
cutting of the inscription on the Craggs monument,
which, owing to the illness of its sculptor, J. B. Guelfi,
was entrusted to Bird, and that his sale catalogues [4]
reveal him as a considerable collector. "Mr. *Francis
Bird*, late of *Lincolns Inn-Fields*, Statuary, Deceas'd,"
possessed casts of works by Bernini, Le Gros, Algardi,
Michael Angelo, Fiamingo, and after the antique, owned
drawings and prints by Dürer, Titian, Michael Angelo,
Raphael, the Caracci, Elsheimer, Callot, Le Brun,
Hogarth, Kneller, La Guerre, Teniers, Vandyck, Breughel,
Sacchi, and Ruysdael, and also a number by Wren,
including his plans for St. Paul's; he also possessed
a quite admirable architectural and antiquarian library.
Among his prints was one of "Cardinal *Richelieu's*

[1] "The Cupola," a poem, 1708.
[2] Now in many cases replaced by modern copies.
[3] I quote from Vertue's transcript; he gives no reference.
[4] Langford, April 30, 1731. I owe the sight of the one known copy to
the courtesy of Mr. and Mrs. Finberg.

monument by Girardon," which had a powerful influence on so much later sculpture.

Bird's monuments are, apparently without exception, devoid of the emblems of mortality characteristic of so much English work. He belonged to the age of the Dean "who never mentioned Hell to ears polite," and to emphasise the physical side of death was not to his taste. Nor does he employ the allegorical figure so freely as his successors in the public favour, Scheemaker and Rysbrack ; rather his aim is portraiture, whether busts, medallions, or figures seated or reclining on their elbow. The bust of Lord Godolphin and its neighbours Busby and Dr. Grabe should be set against the Shovel monument if a fair estimate is to be formed of a sculptor whose works, as Horace Walpole's contempt shows, soon grew old-fashioned, but who was at his best a highly competent artist.

It may be useful to append a chronological list of other sculptors of the period whose work is ignored or inadequately treated in the existing books of reference. The great names of *Fanelli* and *Le Sueur* are here ignored, since space is limited and I can add nothing to what is already familiar save to emphasise the primary importance of their work in bronze, a rare medium for monuments at the period. It is the men who are forgotten or whose work has been misunderstood who are in need of interpretation to-day, if we are to form a fair estimate of the sequence of English art ; and it is hoped that what is here said will at least suggest the wisdom of further research.

Theodore Haveus (fl. 1578), sculptor and architect, executed the monument of Dr. Caius (1573), the Gate of Honour, and a lost and very elaborate sundial for Caius College, Cambridge. He received £33 16s. 5d. for carving the monument and £10 10s. for alabaster and carriage.

William White is known only from the monument of Sir John Newdigate (*ob.* 1612), Harefield, Middlesex, signed and dated 1614, apparently the first example

after Guido of Hereford (p. 13) of an artist's signature
upon a monument.

Francis Grigs executed the Hitcham monument at
Framlingham (1638) ; the Darcy monument at St.
Osyth (1640) ; and the Hawkins monument at Brain-
tree (1645). Possibly an Eastern Counties sculptor
therefore, but known only from these signed works.

" That excellent workman Master *Gerrard Chrismas*,"
as Vertue calls him (*ob*. 1634), designed and in part
executed the splendid monument of Archbishop Abbot
at Guildford, one of the latest examples of its kind,
showing the tester canopy with elaborate ornaments,
the recumbent effigy, and the kneeling sons, much as
Cure or Colt might have rendered them twenty years
before. Other works by the same sculptor should
exist, and in the absence of his large relief of James I
on horseback placed on Aldersgate in 1618, which has
long since vanished, we can only regret that his powers
are so little known to us.

His sons *John and Matthias*, Carvers to the Royal
Navy, and famous for their work on the great ship the
Sovereign of the Seas (1637), seem to have carried out
their father's monument at Guildford, and also executed
the Hawtrey monument at Ruislip (1638) and the
Calthorpe monument at Ampton, the first with a stiff,
quaint pair of busts in an elaborate setting of coloured
marbles and the unusual signature *Johannes & Matthias
Christmas Fratres Fecerunt*, which gives us the right
form of the surname, whose " t " is commonly
omitted.

Of *Edward Marshall* (1578–1675) there is a good
account in the *Dictionary of National Biography* which
will supplement what is here said, and a very bad one
in Dallaway's notes to Walpole's *Anecdotes*. He executed the monuments of William, Earl of Devonshire
(1628), at All Saints', Derby ; of Anne, Lady Cutts
(*ob*. 1631), in her shroud at Swavesey ; of Sir Robert
Barkham, his wife and twelve children (not eight, as
Redgrave says), at Tottenham (1644) ; and, to judge

from their style, the Astley monument at Maidstone
(1639) and the Stanley monument (1638) in Chelsea
Old Church. He lived to become Master Mason to
Charles II, and was buried at St. Dunstan's-in-the-
West three years before his son *Joshua* (1629–78), best
known as the sculptor of the pedestal of the Charles I
at Charing Cross. His elaborately signed monuments to
Dean Hammond (1662) at Hampton Lovett, to Bishop
Warner of Rochester (1666) and Richard Brownlow at
Belton, are interesting; but that to Edward, Lord Noel
at Chipping Campden (1664) is a superbly dramatic
work, with two swathed bodies revealed by the opening
gates of the grave, which recalls the Astley monument
above mentioned, and shows the Marshall family as
masters of the *macabre* in sculpture.[1] He bought his
father's office of Master Mason to the Crown from John
Stone (Walpole Society, vii, pp. 29–30); in 1665–6
was Warden and in 1670 Master of the Masons' Company;
died not long after his father and is buried with him at
St. Dunstan's; the shrouded monument of Lady Dudley
at St. Giles'-in-the-Fields may conceivably be his.

William Latham is best known as the sculptor with
the obscurer Bonne of the fine monument of Archbishop
Sheldon at Croydon, with its recumbent effigy on an
altar-tomb sculptured with a mass of bones and skulls.
Vertue justly called it a noble monument, and its
character is so much reflected in those of Bishops Gunning and Dolben (p. 45) that we may ascribe them also
to Latham. Latham was clearly a rich man, since he
bought a " Venus in Brass from Whitehall Gardens "
in 1649,[2] £556 13s. worth of pictures, etc., at the sale
of Charles I's collections in 1650, and £5,001 on October

[1] The drawing for this belonged to S. Lethullier in Vertue's time. B.M.
Add. MSS. 23071, f. 59a.

[2] He and other purchasers were very badly treated by Cromwell, and
petitioned " the Councell of State " in 1658 for the delivery of their pur-
chases at the Sale of 1649, and " desired yr honrs order whereby they may
receive the sd Goods, they have been great sufferers by the late
Genll Cromwells detaining thereof." The petition is preserved among
the Harleian MSS.

23, 1651, and he further carved the head of the converted Sobieski statue in the Stocks Market.[1]

Thomas Burman (*ob.* 1672), the master of Bushnell, was an assistant of Stone's and executed the monuments of Brian Duppa (1662) in Westminster Abbey and of the Beals—the payments made to Burman's widow in 1675 were given by Walpole—at Walton, North Bucks.

William Woodman executed the Mansell monument (1681), and that of Bishop Monk of Hereford in Westminster Abbey, and a third to John Nicholas at Winchester.[2]

William Vaughan signs the splendid Wynn monument (1671) at Llanrwst.

William Linton executed the Offley monument (1661–78) in Old St. Pancras.

Joseph Catterns signs the Finch and Baines monument (1680) with its charming medallion heads at Christ's College, Cambridge.

T. Davis signs the Levins monument (1682) at St. Mary-le-Bow.

One *Flynton* is known from documentary evidence to have carved the delightful Covert monument at Slaugham (p. 86); though it is unsigned, it is dated 1579, and its author cannot be omitted from this chapter.

The artist's signature even makes its appearance on a few brasses during the period covered by this book. " William Gratwick of East Malling in Kentt his executor " signs that of Roger Gratwik (*ob.* 1596) at Tortington ; Edward Marshall, perhaps the sculptor, that of Sir Edward Filmer (*ob.* 1638) at East Sutton ; Silvanus Crue that of Edward Crue (*ob.* 1666) at Hope, Flintshire —and signs it in Greek ; and that of Lady Mary Mostyn (*ob.* 1653) at Llanrwst is by the same artist.   The increase of professional status indicated by these signatures is very significant.

[1] Vertue, B.M. Add. MSS. 23,069, f. 34; 23,071, f. 42*b*; 23,072, f. 27. The I. Latham who signs and dates the Grandison monument at Oxford may have been his father or brother.

[2] His noble Dodson monument at Cheshunt came to my notice too late for detailed allusion.

CHAPTER XII

SOME REPRESENTATIVE SCULPTORS—II

BIRD, as we have seen, carried on the tradition of the recumbent figure leaning on its elbow, set under niche or canopy, but also varied his poses from the figure seated on a sarcophagus[1] to the half-length medallion portrait[2]; nor did he drop the rich architectural settings derived from earlier days.[3] But the time was at hand when two sculptors, both Flemings by birth, both spending almost the whole of their long and honourable lives in England, were to popularise another and more allegorical style, of which something has been said already. These men were Peter Scheemaeckers, Scheemakers, or Scheemaker—his name grows steadily more English—and John Michael Rijsbrach, who signs all his later works M. or Michael Rysbrack, and looked upon himself as English. Hundreds of the works of each can be named, not to speak of many drawings, some of which are readily identified, and hundreds more are doubtless to be found, besides scores and scores of lost works known from their sale catalogues; it will be seen, therefore, that they were men of no small note in English art, though Flaxman dismissed them as " mere workmen."

Peter Scheemaeckers, Scheemakers, or *Scheemaker* (1690–1771 ?), the elder by a year or two, walked from Antwerp to Denmark, and was reduced to selling his shirts in the process; then he walked to Rome and

---

[1] Dr. Grabe. [2] Congreve.
[3] Notably in the vast monument of John Holles, Duke of Newcastle. All three are in the Abbey.

studied ; then came over about 1716, and became an
assistant first of Bird and then of Plumière, a sculptor
who died young and whose monument to Sheffield,
Duke of Buckingham, at Westminster, Scheemaker and
his fellow-assistant Laurent Delvaux, another Fleming,
subsequently carried out [1] (Plate XXIX). In 1728 he
went off to Rome again with Delvaux, after a period
of considerable success in England, and had William
Hoare to stay with him ; worked very hard both on
antique sculpture and baroque ; made a large number
of models ; and returned after five or six years to set
up a big establishment in Old Palace Yard, Westminster, where he drew around him a brilliant band of
pupils. Finally he moved to Vine Street, Piccadilly,
where he remained till 1771, when he retired from business. The date and place of his death are unknown :
his pupil Nollekens's story that he retired to Antwerp
may be true, but the date assigned, 1769, is certainly
wrong, as his sale catalogue of 1771, issued from Vine
Street, in which he speaks of " retiring," proves that
he was still in London at that date.

Scheemaker was a good man and a devout Catholic,
and his pupils were many and distinguished. Nollekens
and the elder Prince Hoare, the younger brother of his
old friend, Sir Henry Cheere and the younger Van
Ost were among them, and even Banks as a youth was
glad to work in his studio. His etched portrait by
William Hoare gives a delightful impression of the man,
so that it is not surprising to read that Joseph Nollekens
" worked for nearly ten years under his friendly master,
without the interchange of one unpleasant word."
That " little Joey " was so honest that Mrs. Scheemaker
could always trust him to stone the raisins, is a sentence
of J. T. Smith's throwing a pleasant light on the
domestic relations of a prentice with his master's
family in the reign of George II.

Rysbrack, also a devout Catholic and the son and

[1] The models were Lot 15 in the Scheemaker sale of June 6–7, 1771,
when the sculptor was retiring from business.

brother of artists, was a delightful person to whom his friend the connoisseur Charles Rogers devotes some warm-hearted pages of appreciation. Generous, dis- interested, and cordial, Rysbrack won the affection of all who came into contact with him ; and won the verdict too from Horace Walpole, no mean judge, of being " the best sculptor that has come to these islands since Le Soeur." He never went to Rome, but his work in the mixed style of the day is usually admirable, and he could be most impressively realistic. He rose early and worked late, and though at first the underpaid and badly treated assistant of James Gibbs, who, like other architects then and later, had a considerable practice as a designer of monuments, he rose to an independent position, and was held by critics as early as 1732 to surpass Scheemaker himself.

Nor were his interests confined to sculpture. He executed a large number of drawings of the sacred sub- jects for which sculpture then offered no scope, and was a connoisseur of no mean order besides, with a fine collec- tion of Italian drawings for the appreciation of which his marked gift for working in the same medium prepared him. He was a very great sculptor, which Scheemaker just failed to be; but their work runs on such parallel lines that it must be treated together. Both had a marked gift for the historical portrait : Scheemaker's Dryden and Rysbrack's Milton in Westminster Abbey are obvious instances ; both were fond of the pyramidal monument with or without attendant allegorical figures, and executed many works in this taste ; both did portrait statues in contemporary and in Roman dress ; both had a genius for the portrait bust of a contemporary. It is not Scheemaker's fault that his Shakespeare in the Abbey is posing—he had to carry out the design of William Kent ; it is not Rysbrack's fault that his monuments to Sir Isaac Newton [1] and Lord Stanhope to right and left of the choir there have details which one could wish otherwise—Kent, whose finger meddled

[1] Plate XII.

in every pie from architecture to fresco, from laying out Kensington Gardens to designing ladies' gowns, was again responsible.

But these works, as sculpture, are very fine, and if the Corporation of Bristol was right in paying £1,800 to Rysbrack for his equestrian statue of William III, they gave his rival Scheemaker a consolation prize of £50, which was not in the bond, and the Corporation of Hull bought his statue, so that neither had any reason to complain, and their works may still be compared and admired.

To give even a hint of the mass of work executed by both is impossible. Westminster Abbey is full of their monuments, not as a rule their best ; but among Scheemaker's works we may single out for mention and admiration the exquisite attendant figures and masculine dignity of the Chamberlen monument,[1] the terracotta model for the latter at the Victoria and Albert Museum being probably the only such model by this sculptor in a public collection ; the late and dignified memorial to Lord Shelburne at High Wycombe ; and the splendid monument to Judge Page, remembered for Fielding's satire in *Tom Jones*, at Steeple Aston, the appreciation of which might be taken as a test of critical open-mindedness. As for Rysbrack, the monument of the Duke of Marlborough at Blenheim, the Abbey Newton, the Foley monument at Witley, Worcs, and many others mentioned in this little book may serve to show how great a master he was. Loved and respected by all who knew him, he died at a good old age at his house " near the chapple in Vere Street, Oxford Road," as Vertue has it, and was buried at Old St. Marylebone Church near his old employer Gibbs, though his tombstone appears no longer to be there.[2]

Of *Sir Henry Cheere* (1703–81) there is an excellent

[1] Plate XXX.

[2] For Rysbrack and Scheemaker the fullest accounts are still those which I contributed to the *Architect* in 1921-2. Rysbrack is a master of portrait busts, and at times, as in the Sir Hans Sloane, on the main staircase of the British Museum, a rival of Roubiliac himself.

account in the *Dictionary of National Biography*.   Pupil
and for a time partner of Scheemaker, he executed
many monuments in the same style, but the baroque
character of such works as the Sausmarez and Wilcocks
monuments in the Abbey has not perhaps been adequately dwelt upon,[1] nor has his admirable use of contemporary costume in such works as the Sir William
Pole at Shute, Devon, a standing statue in Court dress
for which there is a sketch at the Victoria and Albert
Museum, or the very fine Robert Davies at Mold, in
nightcap and loose gown, been fully recognised.   His
William III in the Bank of England and the Codrington
at All Souls', Oxford, wear, it is true, Roman dress; but
his busts of Dean Aldrich and Archbishop Boulter at
Christ Church are excellent instances of straightforward
portraiture, though, like the All Souls' busts of former
Fellows, they lack the final touch which Roubiliac
would have given.   Still, Cheere's quality and output,
apart from the leaden figure factory at Hyde Park
Corner by which he was latterly best known, are amply
sufficient to explain Sir Edward Walpole's regarding
work under him instead of Carter as promotion for his
protégé Roubiliac, and he remains no minor figure in
our sepulchral art.

There is some doubt about the exact date of the birth
of *Louis François Roubiliac* (d. 1762), but it took place
in 1702 or 1705, probably in the latter year.   The son
of a banker at Lyons, he was apprenticed to Balthasar
Permoser, sculptor to the King of Saxony; then returned to France and entered the service of his fellow-
townsman Nicholas Coustou at Paris.   When that
sculptor was engaged on the old Customs House at
Rouen, Roubiliac left him—owing to religious difficulties,
says family tradition—and came to England about 1726,
to execute a monument; he never again left it, save
for a brief visit to Rome in 1752, until his death in
January 1762.   After a period of obscurity during which
he worked as assistant to Thomas Carter, but executed

[1] Plate XXI.

some admirable monuments, he came to London and did a noble bust of Newton for Newton's nephew Conduitt ; and found a pocket-book which he returned to its owner, Sir Edward Walpole, refusing all compensation, whereupon Walpole introduced him to Cheere and remained his friend and patron to the last. Cheere soon perceived his powers, and recommended him to Jonathan Tyers, proprietor of Vauxhall Gardens, to execute a statue of Handel. This made Roubiliac famous, and from henceforward he was looked upon even by so great a critic as Vertue as one of the three sculptors—the others being Rysbrack and Scheemaker —to whom the new Renaissance of English sculpture, " equal to anything done at any time anywhere," was due. His statues, monuments, and portrait busts are the most remarkable of their age. In portraiture he combined dignity, beauty, and realism to a degree still unexampled in our art ; his monuments range from the simplest tablet [1] to the most elaborate baroque works,[2] and he was the earliest sculptor of his age to emancipate himself completely from the tyranny of the pyramidal background, working in a three-dimensional style and imparting a sense of atmosphere hitherto lacking in our monumental sculpture. In the historical portrait he was supreme, as the great series of busts in the Library of Trinity College, Cambridge, and the still greater Newton in the ante-chapel show. He brought the allegorical figure, when he used it. into closer relation with the subject than his predecessors, and was far more sparing in his use of classical costume ; and his care for detail, his unrivalled treatment of marble, notably in figures of women and children, his incredible skill in catching a likeness, remain supreme to this day. His devotion to his art is illustrated by many stories ; he rose early and worked late, " moulded and

---

[1] *E.g.*   Those to James Sotheby at St. John-at-Hackney and Elizabeth Smith in St. Botolph's, Aldersgate.

[2] Those in Westminster Abbey, and at Warkton, Northants, are the best known. Plates XVI, XXXII.

remoulded " his designs, as his friend Bridgen tells us ;
was extraordinarily reckless in money matters, under-
estimating the cost of his Argyll monument, according
to Farington, by hundreds of pounds ; and died suddenly, a bankrupt, on January 15, 1762.

His contemporaries admired his art beyond measure.
To Cowper's friend Lloyd he was another Phidias ; to
Lord Chesterfield the only sculptor of his day, " the
rest being merely stone-cutters " ; to a nobleman who
met him casually " the great Mr. Roubiliac " ; to Wesley
the only Christian artist of his day, a judgment based
on his Nightingale and Hargrave monuments in Westminster Abbey, with their vivid acceptance of the
current eschatology. Yet to Banks and Flaxman he
and his works were anathema, to Ruskin all that was
odious in monumental art, and to Dean Stanley so
detestable that under his rule the Warren monument
in the Abbey was recklessly mutilated. How and why
this came about I have endeavoured to show elsewhere.
For the rest, the reader had better visit Trinity [1] and
Warkton, Windsor Castle (where his busts of Lord
Ligonier, George II, and Handel may be seen), and the
National Portrait Gallery, and, of course, Westminster
Abbey, though here a word of caution is needed. The
monuments have suffered in tone and surface from the
London atmosphere ; several are very badly lighted ;
one has been mutilated. The Abbey therefore is not
the best place in which to appreciate his art, though
a knowledge of the Nightingale monument at least is
indispensable, and for that knowledge the dropping of
every Gothic preconception is essential. Death, to
the eighteenth century, was the Curse inflicted on
man by his Creator, a thing of fear and dread ;
hence the skeleton form advancing from his vault
and aiming at the young and lovely wife from whom
her husband tries in vain to ward the blow. Un-

---

[1] In default there are the plates in *Roubiliac's Work at Trinity College,
Cambridge* (*Cambridge*, 1924). A life of the sculptor is now (August 1927)
in the press.

10

less we are prepared to understand, we shall not appreciate this astonishing effort of imagination. Horace Walpole did not understand, and called it, as many since have called it, " more theatric than sepulchral " ; Wesley did, and to him it was a sublime rendering of the primary fact of human existence.

Joseph Nollekens (1737–1823).—It is convenient to make a slight departure from chronological order, and to mention Joseph Nollekens, R.A., the younger by two years, before his fellow-Academician Thomas Banks, since Banks is the protagonist of Neo-Hellenism in England, while Nollekens stood in the main on the old ways. Nollekens's father, a decorative painter, lived in Soho, and of the sculptor himself, thanks to the biography by his assistant's son J. T. Smith, we probably know more than of any other sculptor of any age. This is no place to set out his incredible meannesses, his unpleasant personal habits, his doubtful ways of acquiring money by the sale of botched antiques, and his system of underpaying his assistants and over-charging his customers. But we may note that he had a genuine love of art, evinced by a fine collection of sculptors' models, a true perception of and admiration for the works of his older contemporaries Roubiliac and Scheemaker,[1] and, at his best, a real gift for designing a stately monument or, as Dr. Johnson said, " chopping out a bust." His Three Captains in Westminster Abbey is a fine work, his pathetic group of Mrs. Howard and her child at Corby, Cumberland, shows taste and power, and such busts as those of Mrs. Simpson at St. Margaret Lothbury or William Windham at Felbrigg rank with his best portraits. But—and it is a serious drawback—he left his marbles to be executed by his assistants, and he turned out studio replicas of his " stock pieces " Pitt and Fox till they became a weariness of the flesh ; he almost always used skimpy

---

[1] Farington's Diary is instructive on both points ; the Nollekens sale catalogues still more so.

classical drapery for his busts [1] ; and he took no great
trouble with his memorial tablets, which in shape
and detail are often inferior to the works of the earlier
sculptors treated of in this chapter ; the lettering too
is a sad descent from the beautiful script always employed by Roubiliac and Rysbrack, a heritage from
the seventeenth century, when the secret of the art
was known to the humblest village mason.   Entirely
unaffected by Neo-Hellenism, he retained the pyramidal
grouping of his predecessors : it is present in the Three
Captains, in Mrs. Howard, in Mrs. Thrale's uncle Sir
Thomas Salusbury at Offley, and in the very late
monument to Mrs. Coke at Titteshall, which is dated
1805.   That influence and his own Roman training, a
long and conscientious one, are always visible, though
there is little trace of the baroque about his work.   He
lived till December 1823, over fifty years after Roubiliac's death, but his art seems to be a survival of the
style of his master Scheemaker.

   John Bacon, R.A. (1740–99), though five years younger
than Banks, may be treated here in order to avoid
separating Banks and Flaxman.   The son of a poor
but learned and devout clothworker of ancient family
in Southwark, he was an apprentice at Crisp's Lambeth
pottery, and there, seeing the sculptors' clay models
sent to be turned into terracotta in his master's kilns,
resolved to be a sculptor.   And a sculptor he became,
inventing tools and learning to use them by the light
of nature, until in 1769 the Academy Schools were
opened.   He was at once admitted as a pupil, carried
off every honour open to him, and in 1773, by the
kindness of Dr. Markham, afterwards Archbishop of
York, was introduced to George III, of whom he made
an admirable and often repeated portrait bust.   From
that moment his fortune was made.   The King got
him the commission for the Chatham monument in
Westminster Abbey ;   the City gave him a similar

---

[1] The Charles James Fox of 1793 in the National Portrait Gallery is a
rare and delightful exception.

commission at the Guildhall; Guy's Hospital one for
the exquisite monument to its founder; All Souls'
required a memorial of Sir William Blackstone, and
obtained the grand seated statue in the Codrington
Library.

His output was enormous, and two factors entered
into it which require some explanation. On leaving
Crisp's, he had become first apprentice, then assistant, then apparently managing director, in Coade's
Factory of Artificial Stone; and the effects of his
Methodist training left him as devout as his old father
and the intimate of Cowper's friend John Newton, of
John Romaine, and of many other Evangelical divines
of the day. The result of the factory training was that
he became used to the idea of stock patterns for monuments and similar works—his firm was apparently the
first to use illustrated catalogues of its products—and
therefore to the repetition of designs; the result of his
religious views was his preference, in most of his lesser
and a few of his more important works, for figures of
Faith, Religion, Charity, and the like, generally beautiful,
but stereotyped and dangerously easy to imitate. This
does not apply to his portraits, which are always admirably vivid and usually much less conventional as
well as better carved than those of Nollekens or Chantrey,
or to his best works such as the late Pococke and Hope
monuments in the Abbey or the early and exquisite
Guy, as original as a Roubiliac in a different way. His
premature death at the age of fifty-nine was a calamity
to English art, and as Sir Edmund Gosse said long ago,
he is one of the very greatest of English artists. He
never left this country, which makes the French affinities of the Hope and Pococke monuments the more
remarkable; and, hasty and irritable as he sometimes
was, he made a large family very happy. But his
fellow-artists detested him. His courtly manners, his
religious jargon—so it seemed to them, though it was
in him utterly sincere and natural—repelled them;
his world-wide professional success—his works may

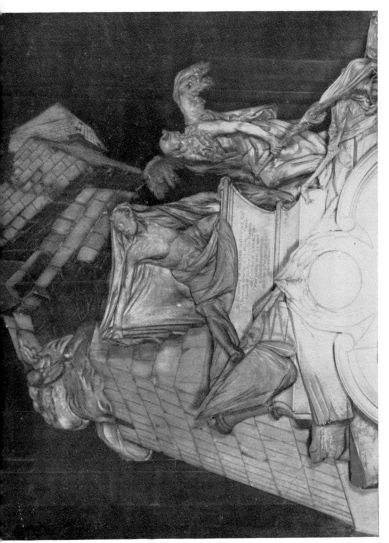

MONUMENT TO GENERAL HARGRAVE, WESTMINSTER ABBEY, BY L. F. ROUBILIAC. THIS VISION OF THE RESURRECTION AS THE PERFECTION OF PHYSICAL BEAUTY WAS TO JOHN WESLEY, ONE OF THE ONLY TWO CHRISTIAN MONUMENTS IN THE ABBEY "AMID HEAPS OF UNMEANING STONE AND MARBLE."

PLATE XXXII.

facing p. 148.

MONUMENT TO JAMES CRAGGS, WESTMINSTER ABBEY.
BY J. B. GUELFI. THE GENIUS OF DEATH BROODS OVER
THE URN CONTAINING THE ASHES OF POPE'S FRIEND;
HIS EPITAPH IS ENGRAVED BELOW.

PLATE XXXIII.

facing p. 149.

be found from India to Jamaica—was aggravating in a man who spoke of himself as a worm ; and his protests that he only looked on his art as legitimate because it might be made to serve the purposes of religion was itself offensive to rivals who saw that art producing an enormous fortune. Moreover, he had a son of the same name who was if anything more devout, who had a large share of the monumental sculpture open to artists during the Napoleonic Wars,[1] and who therefore excited similar feelings when those aroused by the father's success might have died down. Neither sculptor has had anything like his share of recognition from posterity, and though the reader will find any number of works which may belie the verdict that Bacon was a very great, his son at his best a very competent sculptor, he may be advised to hold his hand before condemning them, since their best work deserves all the praise here given.[2] We may add that the statue of William III in St. James's Square, perhaps designed by the father and admirably carried out by the son, is probably the best equestrian statue between Rysbrack and Alfred Stevens.

Thomas Banks, R.A. (1735–1803), was the son of the Duke of Beaufort's land steward. He received a fair education, and at fifteen, as his friend Flaxman tells us, was apprenticed to an ornament carver, working from 6 a.m. to 8 p.m., and then going on to Scheemaker's studio every night for two or three hours' work. He took up sculpture as a profession, became a student at the Royal Academy, and in the same year, 1769, at the age of three-and-thirty, married an heiress, though Reynolds told him it would be the ruin of his art. He was elected to a travelling studentship in 1772 and went off to Rome, where he worked till 1779 on the

[1] India and Antigua are among the places which called for works from the younger Bacon.

[2] For a proof of the younger Bacon's powers, a visit to Little Stanmore, where his father's monument to James Forbes rests on a pedestal carved by him at the age of *sixteen*, will show that what is here said is no exaggeration. Of his mature work the lovely figures on the monument to Captains Hutt and Harvey in Westminster Abbey are examples.

Antique alone, returned to England, and after a short stay went to St. Petersburg, where the Empress Catherine bought his figure of Cupid and scared him home again by ordering a group representing the Armed Neutrality. Once in England, his works ranged from Hellenised scenes like the deathbed of Mrs. Petrie (p. 65) and the dreadful would-be Pheidian groups in St. Paul's to masterpieces like the Penelope Boothby at Ashbourne and the Speaker Chute at the Vyne, Hampshire, in which the English tradition of the recumbent figure in contemporary dress is nobly re-interpreted. His lesser works, monumental tablets and the like, are often good in proportion and his use of Greek detail effective, but his love was given to such subjects as his great Achilles, which, till 1899, was shown at the foot of the staircase of the Diploma Gallery at Burlington House, where his Falling Titan, a powerful and imaginative work on a small scale, may still be seen. He meditated on Plutarch while executing his busts of Horne Tooke and Warren Hastings[1]; the process produced better results than such an attempt at contemporary realism as the Sir Eyre Coote at the India Office. A man of exemplary goodness and simplicity— though his Republican principles once led to his arrest in the stormy days of 1796—he died in the fullness of years and honour, and lies buried at Paddington, near Nollekens and Bushnell. He was the first sculptor to receive the honour of a tablet in Westminster Abbey.

Banks is a most difficult artist to criticise. His reliefs vary from the good to the very bad[2]; his monuments range from the worst taste to the best, his few portraits are good. All that is worst in his art is due to the precepts of Winckelmann. Where he could not, under the terms of his commission, Hellenise, he

[1] One version of the latter is in the National Portrait Gallery, another at the Indian Office.

[2] Thus the Caractacus once at Stowe (model in the Soane Museum) is good ; the Thetis consoling Achilles at the Tate deplorably weak ; the tablet to Baretti in old St. Marylebone church excellent; that to George Clarke at Ickenham bad.

was one of our greatest sculptors ; where Hellenism could intrude, he was capable of anything.

" A competition with the fine forms and beautiful outlines of the antique statues has banished the vitiated outlines of Puget's and Bernini's school," wrote Prince Hoare in 1803, " and our Exhibitions have afforded examples of a pure and correct style." At such a style Banks—sometimes the Wordsworth of our sculpture —aimed, and if his success can be supreme, his failures, as Sir Edmund Gosse has said, are appalling. Captain Burgess, who fell at Camperdown in 1797, stands naked, save for a fragment of drapery arranged in zigzag folds, on his monument in St. Paul's, on one side of a cannon, receiving a sword from the hand of a winged Victory. On the base below are groups of mourning figures derived from Trajanic art, two standing, one seated in front of an ancient galley. Captain Westcott, on his monu- ment in the north transept, in a short tunic sinks into the arms of a Victory about to crown him with laurel ; on the base is a relief of the Nile, of the Vatican, and the Sphinx, framed by two of Banks's detestable palm trees,[1] to show that the scene of Westcott's death was Aboukir. There are not two poorer designs in all St. Paul's. There is no real distinction even in the chiselling, no attempt at composition ; the reliefs have no historical value ; and the allegories, if obvious, have no other merit. Anything less appropriate to officers of Nelson's navy it is hard to conceive ; yet they are the works of a great sculptor working on the theory that the last word in sculpture had been said by the Greeks, and that the only hope for modern art lay in a return to their principles as he understood them. The idea that Greek art was progressive was, of course, unthought-of ; but when Banks could, and did, produce works of the highest order in the traditional English style, it is sad to see him wasting his powers in this fashion. Like Canova afterwards, he was following a shadow ; but at his best he is one of the greatest sculptors we can boast.

[1] That on Sir Eyre Coote's in Westminster Abbey is possibly worse.

We come next to the honoured name of *John Flax-man*. Born in 1755, the son of a professional modeller who kept a shop in Wardour Street and worked occasionally for sculptors of greater repute, Flaxman was a delicate imaginative child with a taste for reading which attracted the attention of his father's customers. Like Banks, he won premiums from the Society of Arts ; like him became an early student at the Royal Academy ; and like him went to Rome after his marriage. But this was not till 1788, and meanwhile he came into touch with Wedgwood, for whom he worked regularly from 1775 onwards. Before he was thirty he was known as a monumental sculptor, and he was early the intimate friend of Blake and Stothard. Patrons began to notice him ; he read Homer in translations ; and two influences, those of Greek and of a definitely Christian art, were noticeable in his productions long before he went to Rome.[1] Once there he worked very hard, and found patrons who commissioned the famous drawings for Homer, Æschylus, and Hesiod. Canova, Schlegel, and Fuseli were loud in his praise ; and he returned to England famous. In 1803 he delivered an address on the death of Banks, in which the principles of Neo-Hellenism were restated, and a violent attack made on the works of Roubiliac, Rysbrack, and their fellows ; and from 1810 onwards, as Professor of Sculpture at the Royal Academy, he dilated upon the same theme.

Technically Flaxman is not one of our greater sculptors. A master of delicate relief, he never grappled with the art of marble carving as his predecessors did, and only one or two of his figures on a great scale— Lord Mansfield and Sir John Ladbroke are notable examples—are really satisfactory. Now and again he achieved much good work in the Greek style, but it is a curious thing that his best work is in the eighteenth-century manner : the bust, of the sixth Duke of Bolton

---

[1] He had completed his *Cephalus and Aurora*, his *Fury of Athamas*, his Venus, Alexander and Borghese Vase, and his Mrs. Morley at Gloucester, showing the ascent of her soul to Heaven, before he left England.

at Basing, is thus incomparably finer than the attendant female figure, a typical Flaxman. Many of his monuments are sometimes sentimental, conventional in a convention largely established by himself, and by no means always well carved ; and a study of them will show that his true vocation was for the silhouette. He rarely gets completely free of the two-dimensional style which his early practice as a modeller for Wedgwood had imposed on him ; but his goodness and simplicity of life and the purity of his work have given him a unique position among our sculptors, and his excellence has become a tradition among many who never think of criticising his more ambitious works in St. Paul's and the Abbey, where they are quite as likely to admire the Nelson or the Howe as the Lord Mansfield, the worse as the better, because Nelson is a popular hero and Mansfield is not.

Flaxman's greatest service to art is as a populariser of Greek ideas. His Wedgwood designs and his outline drawings, based upon Greek gems and Greek vases, are far more Hellenic in spirit than many of his neo-Hellenisms in marble, and while our gratitude for the first may well be outspoken, our gratitude for his more ambitious work is limited by our sense of his incomplete powers as a sculptor, which even his admirer Allan Cunningham admitted, and his false conception of the importance of the Ideal and Typical as against the individual and characteristic. If this may seem too hard a judgment of Blake's " Dear Sculptor of Eternity," it is the judgment of critics who, like the late Sir Sidney Colvin, are ready to recognise his powers and yet speak without hesitation of his inexpressiveness and lack of thoroughness.

One last word as to Flaxman. His lectures, when they dealt with Gothic sculpture, are, said Allan Cunningham, " as rich as a chapter of old romance," and his latest works were Gothic in type.[1] He was, that is, among the pioneers of the love of Gothic art, and it

---

[1] There are good examples in Salisbury Cathedral.

was quite as much this fact as his own achievements
that won him the praise of Ruskin and that curiously
unshaken position in our guide-books, which are still
careful to record even a minor work when an important
monument by an earlier sculptor is dismissed with
contempt because, little as the guide-book suspects
it, Flaxman himself denounced such art in terms of
equal vehemence a hundred and twenty years ago.

The omission of the Carters, Joseph Wilton, R.A.,
and a dozen others from this chapter is simply due
to considerations of space and the fact (1) that other
accounts are available, (2) that they are types of
their age, rather than leaders in the development of
English sculpture. As for the minor men, to attempt
a list of masters of the period not to be found in the
dictionaries were a task too colossal for the scale of
this book. Some, such as Crutcher, Tufnell, Rose,
and Harris, are mentioned in the text ; others, almost
equally interesting, might be enumerated by dozens.[1]
But there is one family whose achievements cover nearly
a century, but are so different in kind that they cannot,
like the products of the Johnson school, be treated
together. Three generations, not two, are involved,
and that at a time when English sculpture was under-
going a complete transformation.

Thomas, William, and Edward Stanton link the
traditional school of alabaster workers with the full-
blown eighteenth-century style, yet no adequate account
of them exists, and of William, the most prolific, not
one word seems to have been written. Walpole briefly
refers to a single work of Thomas, putting it in the
reign of William III instead of Charles I ; Redgrave
to three by Edward ; the rest is silence. Yet Vertue's
note, and the obviously incomplete list of works here

---

[1] Thomas Adey, author of the exquisite Sergison monument at Cuckfield
and the Byde monument at Bengeo, is known otherwise only as sculptor
to the Society of Dilettanti ; John Annis, author of the Foxall monument
at St. Botolph's, Aldersgate, and the glorious W. R. Lytton Strode at
Knebworth, should not have been omitted from the text ; both sculptors
may rank with Rysbrack himself.

given will show their rank as artists, and further research may throw more light upon a studio remarkable
even in the most active days of English sculpture.

Vertue, in describing the church of Stratford-on-
Avon (and, incidentally, noting the fact that he bought
a cast of Shakespeare's monument), writes of the
Combe monument : " in the church . . . a young Man
and Woman, hand in hand—she Judith Combe, (daughter of Wm. Coomb) *ob.* 1649 [resting her left hand on
a skull]. This monument erected about 40 or 50 years
ago, the Sculpture tolerable taste. Tho. Stanton fecit
Holb. Father of William, whose son — Stanton now
living." [1] The work in fact is more than tolerable, an
excellent example of the late alabaster school, whose
conventions naturally perplexed Vertue (Plate IV*b*) ;
more important is the information that we have to
do with three generations of sculptors, all, as we shall
see, working in Holborn.[2]

Of *Thomas Stanton*, sculptor of the charming busts
of the betrothed pair just described, I know nothing else
save his mural monument to Sir Thomas Lyttelton
(*ob.* 1650) at Worcester ; the unsigned monument of
Thomas Windham (*ob.* 1653) at Felbrigg may well be
his, and there is a possibility at least that he was a
brother of the Theophilus Staunton of Holborn, a
member of the Plumbers' Company, to whom, as I
find from their records, John Bushnell's father was
apprenticed about 1621.

William Stanton, son of Thomas, executed the signed
monuments of John Bromley (*ob.* 1674) also at Worcester ; of Charles Holloway (*ob.* 1679) at St. Mary
the Virgin, Oxford, and presumably that of Charles
Holloway, Junior (*ob.* 1698), which closely resembles

[1] B.M. Add. MSS. 230.
[2] I have to thank Canon Melville for a rubbing of the signature, which
is as Vertue gives it. When I saw the work in 1925, the glaring injustice
of Vertue's verdict on its artistic merits was apparent, but may be explained, like Walpole's judgment of Bird, by the difficulty felt by every
generation as to the art of its grandparents, which appears old-fashioned
without yet having become historical.

it ; of Anne Bean (*ob*. 1679) at Hythe ; of Sir Richard and Lady Harrison at Hurst, Berks, an important work representing him kneeling in armour, while she reclines against a stool. There are also fine busts of Sir John and Lady Dormer (*ob*. 1674, 1672) at Quainton ; one of Hugh Saxey at the Saxey Hospital, Bruton ; the Skynner monuments at Hitchin (1669, 1697) ; and a series of altar-tombs at Mitton, Lancs, to Richard Shirburne (*ob*. 1667), another Richard and his wife Isabel (*ob*. 1689, 1663), and a third Richard (*ob*. 1690) ; the agreements are in existence, and show that the works were erected in 1699 and that William was still at Holborn.[1] On the strength of these exquisite works— white marble effigies in the simplest contemporary dress recumbent on black marble tombs—we may safely ascribe to Stanton the similar recumbent effigies of Sir John and Lady Evelyn at Godstone, and those of Jane Done (*ob*. 1662) and her sister Mary Crew (*ob*. 1696) and the delicious little Mary Knightley with her flowers, mentioned in Chapter VII, at Tarporley. The Mitton tombs alone would place this Stanton in the foremost rank of English sculptors (Frontispiece).

He cannot have survived their erection long, since we find his son Edward, whose Christian name Vertue did not know, at work in the first decade of the eighteenth century. His monument at Knebworth to Sir Richard Lytton (*ob*. 1705) gives us his Christian name, *Edward Stanton Londini fecit*, and we can have no hesitation in ascribing two other monuments of the same family in the same chapel to his chisel. Sir George Strode (*ob*. 1707) is signed only *Stanton fecit*, and like the Sir Richard represents him recumbent in a magnificent architectural setting ; the other, Lytton Lytton Strode (*ob*. 1710), though a standing figure, is unsigned.

Closely resembling the Sir Rowland, even to the flanking angels with their gilded wings, last relics of the once-dominant craft of painters and gilders, is the

---

[1] I have to thank the Rector for photographs and descriptions of these noble works.

superb Lord Coventry (*ob.* 1699) at Elmley Castle, signed *Stanton fecit Holb.* Another type of monument is represented by the fine signed bust of Edward Tyson (*ob.* 1708) in All Hallows', Lombard Street; and the Thomas Jones (*ob.* 1715) at St. Alkmund's, Shrewsbury, like the Elizabeth, Lady Capell, at Kew are his also, though there is no portrait. The monuments of Sir John Spencer (*ob.* 1699) at Offley and of Frances Russell at Strensham, though unsigned, strongly resemble the Knebworth groups, and are probably his. His mural monuments, often with twisted columns, are very interesting examples of classical types carried out often in alabaster; among them are Bishop Simon Patrick (*ob.* 1707) at Ely; Owen Bold (*ob.* 1707) at Wrexham, Sir Richard Newdigate (*ob.* 1728) at Harefield, Middlesex, and Bishop Fleetwood (*ob.* 1723) at Ely, the latter being signed *Stanton and Horsnaile, London.*[1] It is clear therefore that Stanton had by then taken into partnership the mason subsequently employed on the Mansion House.[2] Many unsigned works of the same type, notably that of Hester Cotton, *née* Salusbury, erected in 1714 at Whitchurch, Denbigh, may be ascribed to his workshop.

The works here enumerated, noted by myself and my son during the past three years, can only represent a tithe of the output of the family, but they may serve to show both the quality of the sculptors and the astonishing change that passed over English art between the days of the frontal busts of the Combes at Stratford, with their suggestion of the hand of Stone, to the temple-like structures with their attendant angels at Elmley Castle and Knebworth, and the admirably realistic portrait of Edward Tyson. An exhaustive study of the works of the Stanton family would form a fitting subject for a monograph.[3]

[1] There are two more with the same signatures at Belton.

[2] Perks, *History of the Mansion House,* 1922. Index.

[3] This section on the Stantons owes much to the unremitting diligence of my son, who compiled the list of works and sketched many on the spot. I am indebted throughout to his notes and pencil, but nowhere more so than here. A large number of minor works are here omitted.

CHAPTER XIII

CONCLUSION

FOR many centuries the word "tomb-maker" was a synonym for sculptor; the fact is eloquent of the importance of our monuments in the history of English art. Like other arts, it is always developing as the mind of man develops; and that mind expresses itself most fully in monumental sculpture because the commemoration of the dead touches us all so nearly.

We are ready enough to admit the beauty of Attic grave reliefs and Gothic tombs; why do we not take the trouble to understand the monuments of other periods? If our forefathers had done so, we should have been spared some of the worst vandalisms of which the nineteenth century was guilty.

For if Winckelmann's work produced the Hellenic reaction, the Oxford Movement reinforced the Gothic Revival. Post-Restoration buildings, fittings, monuments, became odious to men bent, like Keble, on destroying every relic of the detested age of Latitudinarianism. We talk, and rightly, of the devastation wrought by Puritanism; of that wrought by the authority of the Church itself between 1830 and 1900 we hear much less, because we have been trained to consider Gothic and Christianity as interchangeable terms. Even in the year of grace 1925 an appeal for the restoration of a series of sedilia, involving "the removal of a large Caroline monument" from a Wiltshire church was published in *The Times*; the idea that this removal was itself an outrage never entered the heads of those responsible for the scheme. The appeal to consistency, to what ought to be, has a dangerous plausibility ; but consistency attained by wiping out the past is purchased at a heavy price. Flaxman thought of the fifth century B.C., and produced Professor Sibthorp ; Dean Stanley and Sir Gilbert Scott kept their eyes upon the thirteenth century and removed or mutilated what they disapproved of. They could not too severely reprobate the action of the eighteenth-century dean who wanted to destroy the monument to Aymer de Valence as that of " one of those wicked Templars," and to put Wolfe's cenotaph in its place ; but they had no hesitation in abolishing all the eighteenth-century art that they could and condemning the rest.

We must put ourselves in the artist's place if we are to understand his art. We accept the mediæval sculptor's scheme, his ideas, his proportions, without question, and admire the soul received by angels on the Percy monument at Beverley because it is a mediæval allegory. We look at such an allegory as Roubiliac's monument to General Wade in the Abbey, to expound whose beauties Erasmus Darwin devoted a page of notes in his *Botanic Garden*, and take no manner of trouble to understand what the artist meant ; we condemn it as that sculptor's contemporaries condemned the " Gothick " sculptures we admire, offhand and airily. Truly " ignorance, Madam, pure ignorance," has much to answer for.

The desire to remove the later monuments from Westminster Abbey shown by many superior people to-day is really a proof of their own narrow-mindedness. We should get a Gothic Cathedral no doubt, but it would not be the Abbey, the national resting-place of our great men. For centuries our sculptors have given of their best, each in his own manner, to commemorate our dead : who are we to say what shall be spared and what shall not ? The whirligig of time brings in his revenges, and even the periwig and Roman armour, once we understand them, become not a monstrous freak of the sculptor's but the expression of the spirit of the age in which they were the only wear for persons of importance.

To remove what you and your contemporaries do not like and have never troubled to understand is an easy way of earning popularity—at the time. I was recently talking to a verger in Westminster Abbey about the ominous cracks in the monument of James Craggs, a large and little-regarded structure to the south-west of the nave (Plate XXXIII). "We're thinking of moving it altogether ; nobody likes it," was his reply. This may be unofficial, but it is ominous, an outrage, when we know the facts, and the epitaph itself should make it clear :

> Statesman, yet Friend to Truth, of Soul sincere,
> In action faithful, and in Honour clear.
> Who broke no Promise, serv'd no private End,
> Who gained no Title, and who lost no Friend,
> Ennobled by himself, by All approv'd,
> Praised, wept, and honour'd, by the Muse he lov'd.
>
> A. POPE.

You may follow every stage of the work in Pope's Letters, may note the interest with which he watched its progress, the anxiety with which he records the sculptor Guelfi's illness, the care he lavished on the very lettering when, owing to the illness aforesaid, the cutting of the epitaph had to be entrusted to another hand. The work is the memorial of a great man's love for his friend, a love which spared no care for that friend's tomb. The sculptor, too, is worth knowing, though without a hunt through the Vertue MSS. in the British Museum or a glance at the available accounts of that sculptor's career [1]—for Horace Walpole's notice is the least adequate imaginable—you will find it hard to learn anything about him. He, Giovanni Baptista Guelfi—his Christian names are found upon a

---

[1] My own, in the *Architect* for 1922, is the longest, but it is not complete ; and my note in Thieme-Bekker is disfigured by an error, the attribution to Guelfi of a monument which subsequent research in the Vertue MSS. proved to be by Rysbrack.

bust at Deene—was a protégé of Lord Burlington's, who brought him over from Italy, gave him work and a studio in Burlington House, introduced him right and left, and finally, getting tired of the Signor's airs, packed him off to his native Bologna, where he died in 1734. Guelfi loved youthful male figures in loose draperies leaning upon an urn ; there is another at York Minster, yet another in St. Mary Abbot's, Kensington,[1] and they are unlike English work of the period in that there lingers in them something of the mysticism of the Seicento.

And the tomb on which Pope spent so much love is cracked, and may be " moved "—euphemism in all too many cases for dismemberment. If we realised for what it stood, should we still wish it to go ?

The study of monumental sculpture other than mediæval is hardly yet a science, yet the inquirer need fear no lack of interest. Something strange or unexpected in the work itself, some association suddenly brought to mind, some quality of emotion latent in the type or the inscription, will now and again reward the explorer ; for that to him that hath shall be given is as true of this as of other activities of the human mind.

It may be that the name upon a monument may stir the memory. The first tablet on the left within the great west door of Lichfield Cathedral is to Gilbert Walmisley. Dr. Johnson's noble tribute to the friend of his youth thrills through the brain ; he must have made pilgrimage to it when he came back to his birthplace, and read with Boswell this tribute to his friend, and his friend's wife Magdalen Aston, and her sister Elizabeth.

A mural monument, again, at Hailsham, records the death of many members of the family into which married Richard Plumer of the South Sea House, and of Richard Plumer himself. We remember Elia's " fine, rattling, rattle-headed Plumer," and his pride in his kinship with the house of Blakesmoor in Hertfordshire, and thank the epitaph which gives us a new

[1] To Addison's stepson, Lord Warwick.

link with Elia.   Or, sitting in Archer's noble church at
Birmingham, the eye turns from the great Burne-Jones
windows to catch sight suddenly of a pyramidal monument bearing the name of Edmund Hector ; Dr. Johnson is there with his school-fellow, and page after page
of Boswell rises to the mind.

The church at Hagley is a typical example of Victorian piety ; but by the font still stands a single
monument which recalls one of the great love-stories
of the eighteenth century. On a plain marble base
a weeping cherub, exquisitely carved and holding a
torch reversed, sits by an urn bearing the one word
Luciæ, " To Lucy."   The mind goes back to the poems
in Dodsley which Lord Lyttelton addressed to his wife
when living and to that tender Monody upon her
death which, read or remembered in their setting—
though his Hagley was, when I saw it in March 1926,
but a ghastly ruin—form a new commentary on the lot
of man, and gain a deeper meaning with Lucy's name
before us.

> In vain I look around
> O'er all the well-known ground
> My Lucy's wonted footsteps to descry,
> Where oft we us'd to walk,
> Where oft in tender talk
> We saw the summer sun go down the sky.

Lucy is buried in Staffordshire, but her husband could
not rest without some token of her presence, some
echo of her name, in the church where they had wor-
shipped side by side.

It is a commonplace that we can go nowhere without
meeting friends, or friends of friends ; for the student
of our monuments this is in no common measure true.
Here is a monument at Aston, erected by the eldest
daughter of John Cloberry of Winchester ; the mind
leaps to Sir John's massive figure, life-sized, in periwig
and full-skirted coat, carved by his friend Sir William
Wilson in the Cathedral there.   At Denham lies a Mrs.
Probert whose daughter married " John Baker Holroyd

of Sheffield Place in the County of Sussex Esqr." ; you are linked at once with Gibbon's hostess and with Gibbon himself, who lies in the same mausoleum as the Holroyds in the church of Fletching. Or at Firle you meet the Lady Gage whom three men wished to marry, and whom all three did. The story lingers in the memory ; but when far away, at Hengrave in Suffolk, you meet with the noble figure of the son, Henry D'Arcy, whom she bore to that second husband and lost when he was twenty-one,[1] she becomes a sorrowing mother as well as a heroine of romance.

Now and again a monument may throw fresh light upon English life. It is to the honour of England that a tablet might be erected to some honoured Romanist in ages most intensely Protestant, and as the fact is little realised, one or two instances may be of interest. Among the brasses and imposing monuments at West Grinstead is a mural tablet rich in scroll-work, flowers, and cherub heads in Cibber's manner, bearing the names of Richard Caryll and his wife, the beloved squire of the parish, and then this unlooked-for end to the inscription : " Peter Caryll brother to the said Richard. He was a Religious of the Holy Order of St. Benedict, and dyed 29 of October 1686." The Carylls it was who, to compose the quarrel between the Petre family and Mrs. Arabella Fermor, told Mr. Pope—often their guest in Sussex—the whole story, and thereby created " The Rape of the Lock " ; but it is less their literary interest than the simple words telling of Richard Caryll that come home to us. How dear must the family have been to their neighbours for this " Religious " to have been commemorated in an English church just after the fury of the Popish Plot !

Another Popish burial, at Twickenham, belongs to the world's history. The church, a building of the lovable warm eighteenth-century brick, is in itself delightful, but Pope's monument by Prince Hoare of Bath, erected in 1761 by his editor and adorer Bishop War-

[1] p. 28

11*

burton, is frankly uninspiring. Not so the tablet to
Pope's father and mother, with his own name upon it.
Pope had his faults, his vices even ; but he was surely
as perfect a son as ever lived. All England would have
buried him in state : he knew it, and " would not be
buried in Westminster Abbey." Incredible as it may
seem, Lady Kneller actually requested him to move
his parents' tablet to make room for the vast monument her husband had destined for himself and wished
to place beside his customary pew. Another site would
do as well for old Mr. and Mrs. Pope ; surely the poet
would see it ? See it he did not, and if Sir Godfrey
got his monument in Westminster Abbey (having
previously quarrelled with the sculptor for omitting
his gold chain and medal in the first attempt), Pope's
parents were undisturbed, and when the time came,
their son's name was added under theirs. It is hard to
read the simple inscription unmoved, as one recalls
the poet's will : " As to my body, my will is that it
be buried near the monument of my dear parents at
Twickenham, with the addition, after the words *filius
fecit*, of these only : " *et sibi : Qui obiit anno* 17—
ætatis —." Far lesser men had claimed and were to
claim the Abbey as their right ; to Pope the grave at
Twickenham was a holier resting-place.

Or a famous name may meet you in an inscription
not at first sight interesting, as when Berkeley himself,
" G. Berkeley, S.T.P.," erects a monument to Anne
Wainwright (p. 97), or James Thomson signs a tender
epitaph for a young girl at Southampton, or Garrick
sings the virtues of a country parson buried at Leather-
head among his people. To come on an epitaph by
Pope or Dr. Johnson, long known only in the printed
page, is to add a new delight to literature. These are
the choice rewards of a study which is in itself delightful,
and which is still a field so unexplored that each traveller
makes his own landmarks, and is in his own modest
way a pioneer.

Above all, this is so with the sculptors. Even the

works of men like the Johnsons, Roubiliac, Rysbrack, and Scheemaker are but imperfectly known to us; of Fanelli and Le Sueur more must remain than is recorded; for the lesser men there is almost nothing. Wilton's work, for instance—and he was an R.A. and a personal friend of Dr. Johnson—is still unfamiliar, a few stock pieces apart, and we shall search in vain in the biographical dictionaries for any full account of men like Fisher of York, André Carpentier, sculptor of Chandos-Timon's monument, Thomas Green, or the Stantons of three generations, all the authors of quite first-rate work; of others, such as Griggs, Palmer, Ricketts,[1] Paty, King, William Byrd or Peirce of Deptford, Charles Harris, Richard Crutcher, or J. Rose, we shall learn nothing whatever; yet a study of their works shows that they deserve a better fate.

What, after all, ought monumental sculpture to be? To Ruskin and his school the mediæval effigy was the only type worth considering. So was the Ideal and Typical to the Neo-Hellenist. We know that mediæval monuments were very rarely portraits, but abstract figures of knights and nobles, figures representative of the class, not of the man. The sculptors of the Italian Renaissance, with a portrait to make, aimed at making that portrait as exact as possible, as became the inheritors of Roman and Tuscan tradition; nor did they hesitate to borrow a motive or pattern from any source which seemed to them suitable. Their art was hybrid, but at least it was not sterile; and its descendant became the artistic *lingua franca* of the West until past the middle of the eighteenth century, when deliberate imitation of the art of another age came to be regarded, in theory at least, as essential. But tradition, in monumental sculpture even more than in other arts, dies hard, and the English passion for portraits, commented on by critics so diverse as Hogarth and Haydon, had a profound influence even upon the Hellenists

---

"M[r.] Rickett Stone Carver at Glocester, a Son . . . a hopefull young Man." Vertue in B.M. Add. MSS. 23070, f. 55b.

Banks and Flaxman, so that certain of their monuments combine direct vision with a basis of tradition in a manner wholly satisfying both to the eighteenth century and to our own.

The airy precepts of their school as to the supreme importance of the general and typical as opposed to the individual and characteristic are in fact even more fatal to sculpture than to painting, since its three dimensions call aloud for careful rendering of form. Form can be overdone, and the later Neapolitan school of sculpture, with its insistence on detail of figure under detail of robe, becomes positively meretricious, just as the converse error, the nineteenth-century mourning figure which avoids any suggestion of the human form under the drapery, is detestably prudish. No sculpture can be a living art without that fundamental brainwork on which Rossetti insisted as the basis of poetry, but—and this is the truth which we are always forgetting —what is fundamental to one age is meaningless to another, because the standard of values has altered. We no longer expect a monument to be "an impressive memorial of affection," [1] but we have no right to condemn our ancestors for taking another view. Wordsworth protested against Pope, Flaxman against Roubiliac, and their condemnation had its effect because they were themselves great men. But the literary critic of to-day who takes Pope at Wordsworth's valuation has small chance of a hearing ; and the time will come when Post-Restoration sculpture will be taken on its own merits, not seen through the eyes of Flaxman the Hellenist or Ruskin the champion of Gothic art.

The apostle's business is to preach. It is for the hearer to try his doctrine, and if he is wise, he will know that in sculpture, as in every other expression of the mind of man, there is no Act of Uniformity. For movement is life, in monumental as in other art ; and to judge every movement by the standard of one age alone is to give the lie to life itself.

[1] Britton and Brayley's *Surrey*, ii, p. 330.   This was praise in 1850.

APPENDIX

A RECRUDESCENCE of the theory which sees in certain
English monuments the hand of Bernini makes it desirable,
even after Mr. Maclagan's article in the *Burlington Magazine*
(1922, p. 116), to restate the objections.   In her *Biography
of the Lucy Family* (1862), the then Mrs. Lucy stated that
the Lucy monument at Charlcote (see Index) was the work
of Bernini, that portraits of Sir Thomas and his lady were sent
to Rome for his use, and the price paid was 1,500 guineas.
But the documents have never been produced ; we know
from John Schurman's own account-book that he was paid
for carving the effigy of Sir Thomas ; and the suggestion
(*Archæological Journal*, 1914, p. 65 ff.), that Lady Lucy
would commission a portrait of her lamented husband from
an assistant of Stone's while employing Bernini for her own
is surely unthinkable.   Her grief at Sir Thomas's loss was
overwhelming, as we know from the funeral sermon preached
over her in 1649: had Bernini been involved at all, it would
assuredly have been on his effigy, not her own, and the argument that no English sculptor of the age was capable of
it is falsified by a dozen works of Stone himself, to which
the effigy indeed bears a strong resemblance.

With regard to two other works ascribed to Bernini, the
Kyrle monument at Much Marcle is wholly English in
style, if probably the finest work of its age ; and the lovely
Lady Berkeley at Cranford, which has a certain Italian
touch about it, is certainly the younger Nicholas Stone's.
As the point is not made clear in the Walpole volume, the
evidence may be restated.   Stone's Diary, under November 6,
1638, records that he received from England " 3 scuchions of
armes to be inlayed in marble for the monument of my Lady
Barkley " ; in May and June 1639 he arranged with one St.
Domenico to continue the work, and paid him for what he had
already done (*Walpole Soc.*, vii, pp. 171, 192).   Only the

sculptor responsible for the monument would have received the correct heraldry for the work or arranged for it to be carried out ; therefore the sculptor of the effigy was Stone himself, and its Italian character is explained by his then being in constant touch with Bernini, of whom he has left us some important anecdotes.

Finally, that Bernini could have done any such work is quite impossible. He was a papal servant, who was only permitted to execute the bust of Charles I because that prince was looked on as a possible convert ; " Mr. Baker's " bust, now at the Victoria and Albert Museum, was only obtained with the greatest difficulty ; and England was in the throes of the Civil War when the Lucy monument was erected. The fact that, twenty years later, his nephew Paolo is said to have made the Lady Jane Cheyne at Chelsea is quite irrelevant ; and the argument that the monuments in question were beyond the capacity of English sculptors is amply disproved by the facts (a) that Sir Thomas Lucy's figure is known to have come from a London studio, (b) that the Berkeley monument was the work of an English sculptor in Rome, and (c) that the works of Colt, Cure, the Johnsons, and Stone can show effigies which need not fear to stand beside them. Where documents are unproduced and history is adverse, the theory of Bernini's authorship is dead indeed.

INDEX